CW01664871

Puffin Books
Editor: Kaye Webb

All About Simon and His Grandmother

Simon often goes to stay all by himself with his Grandmother, and together they think up all sorts of splendid games and schemes. Grandmother always has good ideas and is ready for anything, and Simon likes being busy and doing things, too, so they make a good pair.

Grandmother is seventy-seven and has rheumatism, but she doesn't seem like an old lady at all, if practising jumping on roundabouts at the fair is anything to go by, or winning a pig at bowling and keeping it in the kitchen. She can also take a mighty good kick at a football, is terrific on a pogo stick, and mends her own pipes when the plumber is booked up. No wonder Simon loves her so much, especially as she is so understanding over his own misadventures with the oil-can, and the damage Arthur the pig does when they play together in the garden.

These beautifully told, warm-hearted, funny stories will be enjoyed again and again by the children who hear them and the grownups who read them aloud.

Elisabeth Roberts

All About Simon and His Grandmother

Illustrated by
Prudence Seward

Puffin Books

Puffin Books, Penguin Books Ltd,
Harmondsworth, Middlesex, England
Penguin Books Australia Ltd,
Ringwood, Victoria, Australia
Penguin Books Canada Ltd,
41 Steelcase Road West, Markham, Ontario, Canada
Penguin Books (N.Z.) Ltd,
182–190 Wairau Road, Auckland 10, New Zealand

Stories 1–8 first appeared as *Simpey and His Grandmother*; Stories 9–16 first appeared as *Simpey Comes to Stay*

This edition first published by Methuen Children's Books 1973

Published in Puffin Books 1975

Copyright © Elisabeth Roberts, 1967, 1968, 1973
Illustrations copyright © Methuen Children's Books Ltd, 1973

Made and printed in Great Britain by
Cox and Wyman Ltd, London, Reading and Fakenham
Set in Intertype Baskerville

This book is sold subject to the condition that it shall not, by way of trade or otherwise, be lent, re-sold, hired out, or otherwise circulated without the publisher's prior consent in any form of binding or cover other than that in which it is published and without a similar condition including this condition being imposed on the subsequent purchaser

Contents

1 Simon's Grandmother

Simon's Grandmother always had lots of good ideas. A particularly interesting one was when she thought of jumping up and down off her window seat twenty times every day, to keep her rheumatism at bay. She was seventy-seven, and a big woman, and she was glad that at the moment no one lived in the flat below her, because of the thumping. She was a very kind person.

Simon was six. He was generally as busy as a bee, and he liked doing almost anything. Sometimes Grandmother called him Simpey instead of Simon. For once, when he was much younger, he had told her that Simpey-Simon was his favourite nursery rhyme. They both thought that was very funny. Now he was staying with her for a while.

One day, Simon's big kind Grandmother was practising her jumping when they both heard a creaking sort of sound coming from the floorboards, where she had just landed for the seventeenth time. Then, on the eighteenth jump, Grandmother's foot went right through the floor with an alarming crackling, splitting noise, and there she was, stuck, with one foot on the floor and the other (her right one) well on the way to the ceiling of the flat beneath.

She also had a big splinter in her ankle, which had dug right in, rather nastily.

'Oh golly,' she said, 'now I've done it.'

'Oh golly,' said Simon, who thought he wouldn't look at the splinter again.

'I'll tell you what,' decided Grandmother, 'you go and get the big hammer from the kitchen, while I'm getting my foot out. Then you can bang the boards back.'

Simon found the hammer quite easily. It was under the sink, where they had both been battering at the waste-pipe which had been stopped up.

However, he thought that perhaps a few nails might be

useful too, so he opened his Grandmother's tool-box which she kept in the broom cupboard. She had a very interesting collection of things in it. Simon took some time looking at them. Finally he chose a packet of carpet tacks and a large box of drawing-pins.

'Ha,' she said, when he arrived back. 'I've got it out, you see, but the floor's in a bit of a mess.'

Simon put his things down and stared at the big jaggedy hole with interest.

'It won't go back,' he said at last.

'Oh well,' Grandmother replied cheerfully, 'we'll patch it up somehow. But what worries me is that I've lost my shoe.'

Simon ventured a quick look at Grandmother's right foot. The splinter had gone, but the grey stocking was torn in several places.

'Do you think you could get your arm under those boards and rescue it?' she said.

Simon knelt down as near to the hole as he could without hurting his knees on the sharp bits. He bent his head until his nose was right in the opening. This was no good, as he was shutting all the light out with himself. He moved a little, and although he could now use only one eye, he managed to see quite well.

'What about it?' asked Grandmother, who was resting with both her legs up on the window seat. 'Can you see it?'

'I can see a lot of grey.' Simon's voice sounded hollow and echoey. 'There's some bits of wood, I suppose that's the broken floor.' He got up rather quickly and dusted his knees. 'There are two big spiders,' he said. His face was very pink with all the bending down.

'What we want is a torch.' Grandmother heaved herself off the window seat. 'Come on,' she said, 'I've got one in the kitchen.'

Simon followed behind so that he could watch her walk in the strange way that people did who had one shoe on and one shoe off.

'I hope the battery's still working.' Grandmother reached up to the top of the broom cupboard and took down a dusty torch with a long handle.

'What about a bit of string?' suggested Simon. 'We could tie it round the torch's middle and then lower it down through the hole.'

'All right,' agreed Grandmother, 'you have a look in the string box.'

Then they went back to the hole, but it took a long time to get the string tied properly round the torch. While Simon was finding out how to get it just right, Grandmother took out a small red scarf from under a cushion.

'My foot's getting cold,' she said, wrapping the scarf round it.

'I've done it,' Simon said at last. 'It's your turn to look down the hole.'

Grandmother considered the best way of doing this. In the end, she fetched the big eiderdown from her bedroom and spread it about on the floor. It took her a long time to get ready on it. Then she collected the torch from Simon.

'If you see me disappearing down here, grab my legs,'

she said sternly, so Simon moved at once to her feet end so as to be ready.

Then Grandmother let the torch down through the hole carefully first, and her face disappeared after it, just like a swimmer about to go under water. Her grey hair stayed behind.

'Golly,' said Simpey, 'I wonder if those spiders will be frightened?'

Grandmother made quite a lot of noise while her face was down below. Simon could hear her voice rumbling and mumbling, but he couldn't hear exactly what she was saying, and he didn't dare leave her feet, in case they might need holding on to. At last Grandmother's head came up again, and she turned to look at him.

'The torch was fine,' she said.

'Did you get the shoe?' asked Simon.

Grandmother lay back comfortably on the eiderdown. 'No,' she said, 'I didn't. I could see it, but I couldn't reach it. We shall have to consider what's to be done.' So Simon got on to the eiderdown as well and began to think.

A little later, Grandmother began making a funny noise. Simon gave her a little shake.

'Eh? What?' She opened her eyes at once. 'Thought of anything yet?'

Simon shook his head.

Grandmother sat up and frowned. 'It's a pity I haven't a walking-stick – '

'Or a retriever dog,' added Simon.

'Or a pair of very long fire-tongs — '

'Or an arm that was ten feet long – ' (that was Simon).

'Or a monkey – '

'Or an umbrella – ' Simon stopped suddenly.

Grandmother stopped too, and they looked at each other. 'But I *have*,' she said. 'Well done, Simpey.'

The umbrella was many years old and its black silk cover was quite green in places. But it was very long, and the handle was exactly the right shape for rescuing shoes from under floorboards.

'You'll have to do it,' Grandmother said. 'My rheumatism's coming on again.'

'Oh,' said Simon.

'You can lie on the eiderdown. Here's the torch.'

Simon stretched out on the soft, floaty surface.

'I hope I can do it,' he said. 'Oh, I do hope so.'

First of all he switched on the torch and lowered it down the hole. He wound the end of the string round his left wrist. Then Grandmother handed him the umbrella so that the handle was ready to go down first.

'Don't forget about my legs,' Simon reminded her.

'I'll grab you if you move,' Grandmother promised.

So Simon put his head through the hole. He saw the shoe almost at once. It had its back to him, and was lying sadly on its side, as though it had given up all hope of being rescued. Simon stretched out the umbrella and quite gently jiggled the handle until it was firmly curled under the toe part of the shoe. Then he lifted it up slowly and carefully, trying to keep the torch from bumping it. He moved back and lifted his arm higher and higher. Then, as the shoe appeared through the hole, Grandmother bent down and grabbed it.

'Got you!' she said. And then, 'My goodness, it's full of dust!'

Simon sat up. He felt very hot and his left wrist was turning purple where the torch string had been pulling. He undid it and sat for a moment watching Grandmother.

She was sitting on the window seat dusting the rescued shoe with the little red scarf. She blew inside it and then at last she bent and pulled it on.

'That's better!' She smiled down at him. 'Thank you, Simpey, I'd never have got it out without you.'

Simon felt like flying suddenly. He rose quickly and looked at the hole in the floor.

'I could cover it with cardboard,' he suggested. 'Cardboard and carpet tacks, and drawing-pins.'

'All right,' said Grandmother, 'but not now. Simpey, I've got a good idea.'

'What?'

'Let's have tea. You haven't seen the cake I made, and there are some chocolate biscuits.' Grandmother led the way to the kitchen, and Simon followed.

'I wonder if spiders like chocolate biscuits?' he said.

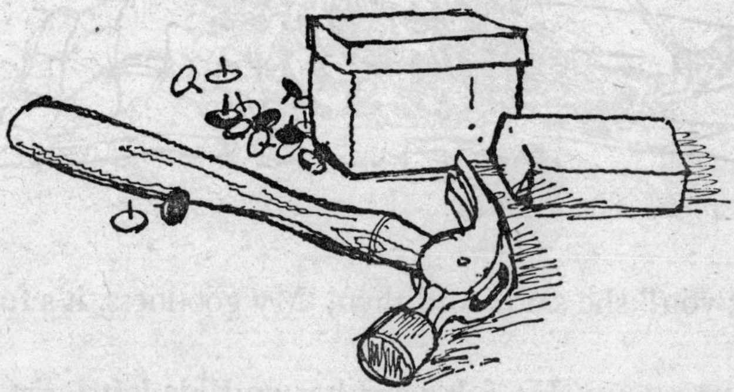

2 The fête

The fête was to start at two o'clock, and Simon and his Grandmother were going. The sun was making the pavements shimmer and the air was so still that the band could be heard for miles.

'One and a half, please.' Grandmother gave the money to a man at the entrance.

'Half a what?' Simon asked, as they walked in to the fête.

'You're the half, and I'm the one,' Grandmother explained.

'But I'm a whole *person*,' said Simon. 'I think that's a bit silly.'

'You're quite right, it's ridiculous,' Grandmother agreed. Then she pointed across the field. 'Look there,' she said joyfully, 'they've got a roundabout. Giddy-up everyone!'

'Giddy-up,' said Simon, and chased after her.

He decided to choose a tiger, and next to him Grandmother sat sideways on a handsome ostrich. There wasn't much of the ostrich to be seen with Grandmother sitting on it, but she looked very fine and imposing, and she couldn't stop smiling.

'I expect all the animals are strong and hearty,' Simon said, as he looked at her.

Then the music blared out suddenly from the centre of the roundabout, and everything began to move.

Simon held tight to the twisty golden pole which went through the middle of his tiger.

'Wheee!' said Grandmother, as they began going round faster and faster, 'I should use both hands, isn't this splendid!'

'You're going up and down when I'm going down and up,' Simon shouted above the din of the music. His cheeks were pink and his hair began to blow about.

Faster and faster they whirled until Simon became very busy holding on. The ostrich flew gaily up and down beside him, nobly carrying Grandmother, and just when it seemed as though they might both take off and fly into space, the roundabout began to slow down and the ride was finished.

Grandmother settled her hat as they both stepped down on to the grass again.

'My word, that was *something*!' she exclaimed.

'My word, it was.' Simon bent down and felt his legs.

'My knees are rather wobbly,' he said.

'Jump about a bit,' Grandmother suggested.

So Simon jumped about until the wobbly feeling went.

'Hallo! What's this?' Grandmother said suddenly. She was bending over a large wooden box which stood in the shade of a big tree. It had wire netting nailed over the top of it, and something was scuffling about inside.

Simon rested his nose on the netting and peered in.

'It's a pink pig,' he said softly. 'It's very small, nearly as small as a kitten.'

Grandmother looked at the notice nailed to the tree. 'Bowling for the pig,' she read out, 'win him for five pence. Huh!' she said scornfully. 'A likely story.'

'What kind of bowling?' asked Simon. His nose had a red ring on it from the netting.

'They have wooden bottles to knock over, like skittles.' Grandmother began to walk on quite quickly.

'But – we can play *that.*' Simon frowned deeply. He ran after Grandmother and caught her sleeve. 'You're better at it than I am,' he said urgently. 'Come *on.*'

The man at the bowling stall looked surprised when Grandmother handed him her five pence.

'I should take it easy if I were you dear,' he said, as he handed her three large wooden balls.

'Nonsense!' Grandmother looked quite annoyed. She lifted her chin and made herself look very tall. She handed Simon her bag to hold.

'Now then,' she demanded, 'where do I stand?'

The skittles looked a long way away. Simon held tight to the bag and bent his head till he could only just see through his eyelashes.

'Well,' said Grandmother, hitching up her skirts, 'here we go!'

Her first ball hit a bump in the grass and missed the skittles altogether. Almost at once she took aim and sent her second ball hurtling down at such a rate that only two skittles were left standing.

'Cor!' said the man.

'Now,' said Grandmother, breathing hard.

Simon shut his eyes completely. He opened them to see all the skittles flat on the ground. Grandmother was rubbing her arm and whistling a little tune under her breath.

'Well I never!' said the man.

'So what about the little pig?' Simon asked him.

'Well now, we have to wait till the fête closes,' said the man. 'It's not many that knocks them *all* down, though, so I'll just take your name and address. It's the one with the best score that wins the pig.'

'Oh.' Simon nodded to himself. 'It would be nice to call it Arthur,' he said. Then, 'I've eaten a bit of your handbag,' he told Grandmother, as he gave it back.

Grandmother chuckled. 'Let's go and get some ice-cream,' she suggested.

That evening they sat together on the window seat in Grandmother's flat. They had seen every bit of the fête. Her feet were in a comfortable bowl of warm water. Simon wore his dressing-gown and they were eating milk and biscuits. It was at that moment that a little van drew up outside the house. Simon looked out. Then he put his mug down carefully on the window ledge.

'Grandmother,' he said slowly, 'you'd better put your bedroom boots on at once. I think our pig has come.'

And it had.

The two men who brought it left the box in the kitchen. Before they went Grandmother spoke to them at the front door for quite a long time. When she came back, Simon's nose had a red ring on it again.

'Would *you* like to let him out?' he said. 'You did the skittling.'

Grandmother looked round the kitchen thoughtfully.

'All right,' she said. Then she bent down and unfastened the wooden door at the side of the box. Almost at once, the pig's pink sniffy face looked out. Simon smiled. He opened his arms wide and went towards it.

'Arthur,' he said. 'Hallo, my little friend.'

Arthur seemed very excited at the idea of making friends. He shot out of the box and darted across the kitchen. His tiny feet made tippy-tappy sounds on the linoleum. Suddenly he stood quite still and looked up at Grandmother.

'Eek!' he said.

'Hallo, Arthur,' Grandmother said kindly.

'Eek! Eek!' said Arthur.

'He's got a good loud voice,' Simon said.

'Yes.' Grandmother stepped round Arthur carefully and went to a cupboard. 'I dare say he'd like a little something to eat,' she said.

'I dare say he would,' agreed Simon.

In the end they all had some porridge. Arthur had his in a tin plate that wouldn't stay still. He began eating at one end of the kitchen floor and finished up at the other. He was a very quick eater. Grandmother mopped the floor.

'I don't suppose he'd want to play anything just now?' Simon said.

'I think,' said Grandmother, 'it would be a good idea if he went to bed early. He's had a very tiring day.'

'He doesn't look very tired.' Simon gazed at Arthur who was sniffing in a corner.

'You can't tell with pigs,' said Grandmother.

'Are you sleepy, little pig?' Simon asked.

Arthur sat down.

'I'll find him something to lie on,' said Grandmother, 'then tomorrow he'll be ready for anything.'

'Tomorrow.' Simon smiled at Arthur. 'My Grandmother's a very good bowler,' he said.

3 Simon's friend

'Arthur, Arthur, Arthur,' said Simon the next morning, as soon as he woke up.

'You'd better hurry,' Grandmother called, 'we've been waiting ages.'

They all had breakfast in the kitchen. Arthur the pig began chasing his plate again.

'Your egg is getting cold,' said Grandmother. 'You can talk to him afterwards.'

Simon picked up his spoon. 'I heard him in the night,' he said. 'He was squeaking and scrumbling about.'

'*I* was doing the scrumbling,' said Grandmother, 'he's a very lively pig.' She yawned a little. Then she said, 'About Arthur – '

'Arthur, Arthur, Arthur,' Simon was eating at a great rate.

'Yes, I'm glad we won him,' continued Grandmother, as she moved the cherry jam across to Simon. 'The only thing is,' she went on, 'I don't think he can stay very long.'

Simon put down his spoon.

There was silence in the kitchen, except for Arthur, who was sniffing loudly under the table.

'Why not?' Simon asked. His breakfast felt as though it was stuck half-way down.

'Ha – well, it's the flat, you see,' said Grandmother. 'I'm not really supposed to keep a pig here at all.'

'I suppose it's the scrumbling in the night,' Simon said. He was twiddling his spoon over and over on the tablecloth.

'Yes. Besides,' said Grandmother, 'pigs ought to live with other pigs.'

'But – ' Simon began.

'*But*,' Grandmother said firmly, 'I've had a good idea. I'll tell you all about it.'

Then she explained that one of the men who had brought Arthur had a splendid farm, not very far away. He had said that the little pig could live there, and Simpey and his Grandmother could visit him whenever they liked.

Simon sat up. 'Has he got other pigs for Arthur,' he asked, 'and horses and cows and a hayfield?'

'The lot,' said Grandmother.

Simon reached for the cherry jam.

'He's going to be a lucky pig,' he said, 'living on a farm, and us visiting him all the time.'

'You've got a whole day before he has to go,' said Grandmother. 'The man isn't coming until after tea.'

'I'm going to teach him to play soldiers.' Simon rested a foot on Arthur, who was rubbing his back against the chair leg.

'The garden would be a good place,' Grandmother suggested. 'He can't get out of there.'

Simon looked surprised. 'But he wouldn't *want* to get

out,' he said, 'not if he was going to play soldiers.'

After breakfast, Arthur followed Simon into the bathroom. At once he wriggled in behind the clothes basket.

'You're a terrible sniffer,' Simon said, as he rescued him. 'Please wait, Arthur, I'm hurrying with my washing as fast as I can.'

But Arthur didn't seem to like waiting very much. His feet never stopped tippy-tapping over the bathroom floor, and his button nose never stopped sniffing. Simon wasn't very long with his washing. He helped the water to run out of the basin, and then turned on the taps and filled it up again. He wet his green face flannel and squeezed it between both hands, till only a few drips came out.

'Now,' he said to Arthur, 'it's your turn.'

Arthur didn't seem very used to washing. He gave a little shriek as the face flannel went over his eyes. Then he tossed his head crossly and backed away.

'Don't be frightened,' Simon said kindly. He picked the flannel up and followed the little pig under the basin.

There was a lot of water about when Grandmother opened the bathroom door. Arthur was looking crosser than ever.

'Ah,' she said, 'there you are. Are you washing the floor?'

'Arthur is now perfectly clean,' Simon said, 'except his teeth, he wouldn't let me find them.'

'My word,' said Grandmother, looking down, 'what a bright, sparkling pig you are.'

Arthur gave a grunt and pushed rudely past on to the landing. He seemed glad to be out of the bathroom.

'I expect he's waiting to play soldiers.' Simon drooped his face flannel over the bath and hurried out to find the toy box.

Grandmother kindly carried Arthur down the stairs and into the garden. As well as the box with the soldiers in it, Simon brought two cannons and a very smart red cushion.

'It's to fall on when we get killed in battle,' he explained, as he saw Grandmother looking at it.

'I don't think red is a very good colour,' she said. 'The enemy could see it for miles.'

'I never thought of that,' said Simon.

Grandmother picked up the cushion. 'I'll throw you another one out of the window,' she promised.

Simon took out his soldiers and counted them. There were eleven and a half. The half was only legs, so he put it back in the box.

'Come here, Arthur,' he said. 'You'd better be the enemy.'

Arthur had found a fascinating spot to sniff at under the hedge. He seemed rather annoyed at having to leave it. However, Simon arranged the eleven soldiers and the two cannons at one end of the lawn, and put the little pig at the other. Arthur fixed his eyes on the soldiers and squeaked mournfully.

'You can have one of the cannons,' Simon said quickly, changing it over. 'That'll be fairer.'

Just then a voice hailed them from above. Simon looked up and saw Grandmother leaning out of her window. She was waving a green cushion.

'Look out below!' she called, and let the cushion drop.

It landed with a loud 'smack!' in the middle of the battleground, and that was enough for Arthur. He scuttled over to a flower-bed and hid behind a fat geranium. Nothing would make him play at soldiers again.

'Oh well, it's a pity.' Simon was putting everything back in the box once more when Grandmother arrived in the garden.

'I've brought you both a bit of apple,' she said.

Arthur came out at once from behind the geranium and chomped up his piece very quickly.

'I think he's a bit young to play soldiers,' said Grandmother. 'Let's both sit on the cushion for a little and think of something else.'

But Arthur knew exactly what *he* wanted to do, and while Simpey and Grandmother were trying to fit themselves on to the cushion, he did it. He dug a big hole under the geranium with his small pink nose.

'Hoy!' Grandmother called to him, when she noticed.

'Hoy.' Simon got up and tried to push the geranium back.

But Arthur was in a very pig-like mood. The only thing he wanted to do was to dig.

The garden was looking very untidy indeed when Grandmother decided they'd better all go inside again. Simon did his best to amuse his friend. He got out his clockwork train set, but Arthur kept tripping over the lines. He tried playing hide and seek, but Arthur always looked when he shouldn't. He tried playing at dressing-up, but Arthur wouldn't.

'All this is very tiring,' said Simon.

It was nearly tea-time when Grandmother finally came to the rescue.

'I've just remembered,' she said, stepping over all the things on the floor, 'I *think* that pigs will sit quietly if you scratch them behind their ears.' She bent down and tried it.

Arthur was delighted. He closed his eyes and was ready to be scratched for ever.

'I'm glad he's stopped rushing about,' Simon said.

So they took it in turns to scratch Arthur until the man from the farm came to collect him. Then they helped him gently into his box, with two apples for company. They waved from the window as the van drove off.

'We'll go and see him soon,' said Grandmother.

'I hope he'll be a happy pig,' said Simon, 'because he doesn't know how to play at *anything*.'

4 The present

'Heigh-ho,' said Grandmother one morning, 'the summer's nearly gone.' She turned over the page of the calendar hanging on the kitchen wall.

'Heigh-ho,' said Simon. 'I wonder where it's gone to.'

He looked up at the new picture on the calendar. 'Old brown trees are not very interesting,' he said. 'The picture with the flowers was nicer.' Then he noticed a red circle round one of the numbers. 'Somebody's been drawing on it,' he said.

'I did it,' Grandmother said. 'That's the date of my birthday, and I didn't want to forget it.'

Simon looked astonished.

'But you're *supposed* to forget it,' he said. 'It's only other people who have to remember it, and then they give you a surprise.'

'Do you know, I never thought of that.' Grandmother looked at the calendar again. 'I don't think the mark will rub out,' she decided, 'but I'll try not to notice it.'

But Simon wasn't listening.

'Could I have a rather strong bag?' he asked suddenly.

'I don't know,' Grandmother said. 'I'll have to look.' She rummaged in her paper drawer. 'What about this?' She held up a large bag which said 'Self Raising Flour' on the outside.

'That's exactly right,' said Simon. 'Now I have to go and put something in it.'

'Don't forget we're going into town this morning,' Grandmother reminded him. 'The bus goes in ten minutes and you'd better wear your blazer.'

'I know,' Simon said, as he darted out of the kitchen, 'that's why I've got to do what I'm going to.'

Grandmother went into her bedroom to get ready. She was some time pinning on her hat. She put on her coat, took a last look round, and picked up her red hold-all. Then she opened the front door of the flat.

'I'm about to go,' she said loudly and firmly.

Almost at once Simon hurried out of his bedroom. He was wearing his blazer and was having to use both hands to clutch the bulging flour bag against it.

'Good gracious!' said Grandmother. 'Whatever is that full of?'

'It's my saved-up pennies,' said Simon. His face grew pinker. 'I need to take them with us, because I've got to buy something.'

'I see.' Grandmother hastily opened the hold-all. 'You'd better put the bag in here for now,' she said. 'We're going to have to run to catch that bus.'

When they reached the town, Simon and Grandmother each took a handle of the hold-all. With Grandmother being so much taller, this was a very uncomfortable arrangement. The heavy flour bag chinked between them.

'Perhaps we could spend the pennies soon,' Grandmother suggested. 'What exactly do you want to buy?'

'Well,' said Simon, looking at his toes, 'it's a present I have to get for someone. I think a sort of toy shop would be best.'

'A present? Splendid!' Grandmother said at once. 'I know just the place. Let's get a move on.'

They bumped their way through the crowded streets, entered a big store and went up in a shining lift.

'Golly!' gasped Simon, as they got out. 'This is a *place*!'

'It certainly is,' agreed Grandmother. 'Give me the hold-all while we look about.'

Simon didn't know what to notice first. There were games and puzzles, kites and balloons, and huge stuffed animals; whole heaps of marbles, drawing and painting sets, and wonderful toys reaching as far as he was able to see.

He was prodding a fat pair of boxing gloves when he noticed Grandmother standing further along at one of the counters. She was fitting a toy arrow into the string of a small bow. As he watched, she lifted it and took aim at a light bulb over her head.

'Grandmother!' Simon said in a surprised voice.

The arrow left the bow quite suddenly and whizzed up to the ceiling. It missed the light bulb, made a small dent in the plaster, and fell down behind the counter. Grandmother smiled kindly at the startled assistant, as she handed the bow back.

'I'm so sorry,' she said, 'I didn't think it could travel so far. It must be a very good bow.' She picked up the hold-all and moved on.

Then Simon found some Red Indian tents. They were bright yellow and had feathers round the top. He bent his head and crawled inside one of them. Then he sat down and crossed his legs for a moment. He felt very comfortable.

'*That* would make a good present for someone,' Grandmother suggested, as he came out.

Simon stroked one of the feathers gently and looked at the tiny entrance in the side of the tent.

'It wouldn't fit the someone I'm getting the present for,' he said at last, 'but it's a pity.'

So they left the tents and went on. Suddenly Grandmother stopped and pointed.

'Look!' she said excitedly, 'over there! Good gracious, I haven't seen one of those for years!'

'Good gracious, one of what?' asked Simon, as she hurried across and took something from a rack on one of the walls.

It was a long metal pole, painted bright red, with two little rubber feet placed on either side of it near the bottom.

'It's a pogo stick,' said Grandmother delightedly. 'It's got a spring inside it, and you can stand on the feet and jump up and down.'

'How, exactly?' asked Simon.

'Ha – well,' Grandmother paused. Then she beckoned to a young man behind one of the counters. 'Do you mind if I try this?' she asked him.

'Er, it's rather – ' the young man stopped and looked doubtfully at Grandmother.

'Thank you very much,' she said briskly. 'Look after the hold-all, Simpey.'

Simon never saw exactly how Grandmother got *on* to the pogo stick, but somehow she gripped the pole and leapt up nimbly, and there she was, standing firmly on the two little rubber feet. Then away she went, springing up and down, round and round, thudding and banging on the wooden floor, her face beaming and her hat slipping slowly sideways.

'Look at *that*!' said the young man.

Several other people stopped to look too.

'That's my Grandmother,' said Simon.

Soon afterwards Grandmother stopped jumping and let Simon have a turn on the pogo stick. He found it very difficult, and kept falling off. Then he did three jumps with the young man holding the pole.

'All you need is practice,' said Grandmother, who had stopped puffing. 'You could leap like a kangaroo in no time.'

Simon decided suddenly.

'*This* would do for the present for someone,' he said.

'I thought it might,' said Grandmother.

So Simon gave the young man the floury bag of saved-up pennies, and Grandmother said she'd go over to the cash desk to help him count them. And then, because the pogo stick was a nuisance about poking people, they decided to take it home.

As they entered the flat, Simon said suddenly, 'Grandmother, I've got a surprise for you.'

'Oh?' said Grandmother.

'It's about this pogo stick.' Simon clutched it tightly and his ears were as red as fire. '*You're* the someone it's a present for. It's not your birthday, but we can hide it till it is. I thought I might forget if we didn't buy it today.'

'Oh, Simpey,' said Grandmother, 'what a *lovely* present.' She got down on one knee to thank him better.

'I got it because you seemed to be liking it in the shop,' said Simon, looking pleased.

'But I never thought anyone would ever give me one,' Grandmother said happily. Then she said, 'I'll tell you what, Simpey.'

'What?'

'As soon as it's been my birthday, you can borrow it whenever you like.'

'*Golly!*' breathed Simon, and he took it away to hide it under his bed.

5 Simon's idea

Simon's Grandmother was looking inside her dark little cupboard on the landing.

'Dear me,' she said, 'there's a terrible lot of rubbish in here. I must tidy it out.'

'What kind of rubbish?' said Simon.

'You never know till you look,' said Grandmother, poking at a dusty brown-paper parcel.

'*I* could tidy it out,' Simon suggested. He poked at the parcel too.

'That's an idea,' Grandmother said at once, 'and I'll do some baking for tea.'

So Simon got down on his knees and began directly. First of all he took out the brown-paper parcel and felt it all over. It was quite heavy. But he couldn't undo the string to see what was inside it, so he left it till later. The rest of the things in the cupboard were mostly old tins of polish and brushes and didn't look very interesting, but he thought he would empty it, just in case.

It was quite a time before Grandmother came to look for him again. She stepped over the heap of things on the floor and peered into the cupboard. Simon was squashed inside it.

'Ah,' said Grandmother, 'how are you getting on?'

'I've finished,' said Simon, undoing his legs. He pointed to the brown-paper parcel. 'Some of your rubbish is quite interesting,' he said. 'Can we go and open this?'

Grandmother looked at the muddle on the landing.

'How about putting all this back in the cupboard first?' she suggested. 'You begin, and I'll look for the scissors.'

'All right,' Simon gave a deep sigh. 'But I only said I'd tidy it *out*,' he said. 'I thought someone else would tidy it in again.'

'I've made some very superior chocolate buns,' Grandmother said over her shoulder. 'You can have one when you've finished.' Simon was finished quite quickly.

'Here's the parcel,' he said, bringing it into the kitchen. 'Those buns smell very chocolaty, don't they?' he added.

So Grandmother gave him one and then began snipping the string with her big kitchen scissors.

'There!' she said, as the last piece of wrapping fell off the parcel. 'How about that!' She placed a big brass hand-bell on the table.

'Golly,' said Simon, 'what a very useful thing.'

'I bought it a long time ago,' Grandmother said, 'for the pigeons.'

'How do you mean, the pigeons?' Simon asked. He curled his hand round the smooth wooden handle.

'They kept eating my vegetables,' Grandmother explained, 'so whenever I saw one, I clanged the bell at it out of the window, and off it went.'

'Clang, clang,' said Simon in a deep voice. Then he said, 'Do you think you could pretend to be a pigeon now?'

'Just for a moment,' Grandmother said.

So she went into a corner and pretended to be one. Simon clanged the bell to and fro till his arms ached and the cups rattled.

'Stop! Stop!' cried Grandmother, flapping her arms up and down.

'I've flown away, I've flown away!'

'What a pity,' said Simon, stopping. 'So you have.'

Grandmother flopped into a chair, and said, 'I expect the bell could do with a rest.'

'Yes,' said Simon, 'I can give it another little ring later.'

'You know,' Grandmother said, 'I expect that bell used to belong to someone like a schoolmaster, or perhaps a muffin man. It sounds *much* better when you ring it outside.'

'I suppose there'd be more room for the noise,' said Simon. 'What are muffin men?'

'Well, there aren't any now, but they used to sell muffins,' said Grandmother, 'a sort of thick, flat, crumpety thing. They carried them through the streets on trays, and clanged a bell to let people know they were coming. It was an exciting sound.'

'Muffin, miffin, moffin,' said Simon.

'It saved a lot of bother,' Grandmother said. 'People ran out and bought the muffins, toasted and buttered them, and hey presto! there they were, all ready for tea. Oh well – ' Grandmother got up. 'Now I'd better get on. I've got my little read at the paper to have yet.'

'I could be giving the bell a good hearty polish while you're reading,' said Simon.

'So you could,' Grandmother said. Just before she went, however, she decided to put the chocolate buns in a tin. 'In case there are any flies about,' she said.

There were a few stale rock cakes left over from the week before, so she took them out and placed them on the draining-board.

'They're as hard as a brick,' she said, 'but we'll save them for the ducks in the park tomorrow.'

'As hard as a brick,' Simon said, when Grandmother had gone. He banged the rock cakes up and down several times.

Then he fetched the polish and a duster, and put the bell on a newspaper on the kitchen floor.

'You nearly keep clanging by mistake,' he said to the bell, and began polishing.

When the bell was as bright and shining as the sun, Simon practised making faces in it. It was then that he had his idea. So he thought he would go and see if Grandmother was still reading her newspaper.

He put his head quietly round the sitting-room door and had a look. Grandmother had her feet on a stool and was stretched out before the fire. The newspaper lay across her face. It was blowing gently up and down.

'Good,' Simon said, hurrying back, 'she is.'

The sitting-room clock was chiming five when Grandmother sat up with a start. The newspaper fell on the floor.

'Jumping monkeys!' she said loudly. 'What on earth is that terrible noise?' She pushed herself up out of the chair and went over to the window.

A small figure was standing down in the garden. It was Simon. He held the brass bell with his two hands and was heaving it to and fro, to and fro, filling the air with such a clanging and clattering that Grandmother hastily opened the window.

'Hey!' she called, waving vigorously to attract his attention.

Simon saw her and put the bell down. Then he picked up what looked like the kitchen tray. 'Muffins for sale, muffins for sale,' he sang out in a high sort of voice.

'Eh?' Grandmother looked startled. 'Oh, I see.' She put her head further out of the window. 'I'll take half a dozen,' she shouted. 'But bring them up straight away!'

'I've only got two,' said the muffin man, 'but I'm coming.'

Grandmother made the tea and obligingly toasted and buttered the two humpy lumps that Simon took off his tray.

'How did you make them?' she inquired.

'They were easy,' Simon said. 'I borrowed two of the rock cakes and squidged them about with some water.'

'Fancy,' said Grandmother. Then they took the tea, the muffins and chocolate buns through to the other room and settled themselves beside the fire.

After a while Simon said:

'You've dropped a big piece of muffin down the side of your chair.'

'Oh, have I?' said Grandmother, rescuing it. She took a big drink of tea.

Simon took a small bite out of his muffin and then put the rest of it down on his plate.

'I know why there aren't any muffin men any more,' he said.

'Really? Why?'

'Because,' he said slowly, 'I expect people would much rather have chocolate buns.'

Grandmother smiled cheerfully.

'You're quite right,' she said. 'Why not pass them over?'

'I expect,' said Simon, 'the ducks will be *very* interested to try a muffin.'

6 The bonfire party

Simon and Grandmother were enjoying themselves in the park. Simon was busy borrowing the pogo stick he had given Grandmother for her birthday, and he was getting quite good at jumping on it. When he first began, he kept banging his nose on the long handle.

'This pogo stick is very hard,' he said, stopping for a while.

'Come here a moment,' said Grandmother, 'I've had a good idea.'

She took Simon's blue woollen muffler and cleverly tied it round the pole, just where his nose reached to. After that things were much better. Soon Simon managed to jump in the air three, and at last four times, one after the other, before he fell off.

'First rate!' Grandmother said, helping him up. Then she gave him back his muffler. 'It's getting chilly,' she said. 'You'd better put it on now and we'll go home for tea.'

When they reached the park gates Simon was rather out of breath.

'I wonder who's going to carry this pogo stick,' he said.

'Half a moment,' said Grandmother, 'there's a new notice on the gates. I wonder what it says?'

Before she could read the notice, however, Grandmother had to put on her spectacles and stand quite close to it, for the afternoon light was already fading and the printing was difficult to see. Simon was tasting the handle of the pogo stick while he waited.

'Well I never!' Grandmother sounded surprised. 'Just listen to this! "Firework and Bonfire Party",' she read out. '"To Be Held In The Park On November 5th. At Six o'Clock. Admission Ten Pence. Everyone Invited".' She stepped back and looked down at Simon. 'What do you think of *that*!'

'I don't know yet,' said Simon. 'Are we going to it?'

'Rather!' said Grandmother. 'It's a long time since I went to a firework party. I shouldn't like to miss this.'

'Your pogo stick is very heavy,' said Simon, who kept tripping over it.

Grandmother chuckled. 'Give me one end, and you take the other,' she suggested, 'then we'll be home in no time.'

On the morning of the bonfire party, Grandmother and Simon went shopping.

'We'll buy a few fireworks to take with us,' said Grandmother. 'Come along, they've got some in here.'

Inside the shop, Simon rested his chin on the glass counter and stared at the rows and rows of fireworks underneath it.

'They all look very bangy,' he said.

But Grandmother spoke to the man behind the counter.

'I'd like six packets of Sparklers, please.'

'Yes,' said Simon at once, 'I like Sparklers.'

When they got home, Simon arranged the packets in a row on the kitchen table.

'It's a long time till six o'clock,' he remarked.

Grandmother looked thoughtful. 'The curtains in the sitting-room are very thick,' she said. 'If we drew them, the room would be quite dark. Then we could try one Sparkler each.'

'I'll open a packet,' said Simon.

They drew the curtains as carefully as possible, but still quite a lot of chinky bits of daylight kept coming through.

'There's a nice dark corner behind this armchair,' said Simon, who was sitting there.

So Grandmother brought a box of matches and squeezed in beside him. Then she lit the Sparklers.

'We won't wave them about,' she said. 'There's not very much room here.'

So they both held out their arms carefully while the fireworks fizzled and spluttered, filling the corner with dazzling light.

'I knew I liked Sparklers,' said Simon, blinking, when they finally went out. He gave Grandmother what was left of his, and then helped to push her up off the floor.

' – And there's hundreds left for tonight,' he said, hurrying back to the kitchen.

At six o'clock that evening Simon and Grandmother joined the little crowd of people who were gathered round the huge bonfire in the park. This had now been carefully lit by two of the park-keepers, and was already snapping

and crackling as the flames licked round the dry twigs at the bottom of it.

'Hurray!' cried Grandmother, waving the bag with the Sparklers in it as an extra big flame shot up the side of the bonfire. Simon pulled at her coat.

'I think we ought to move back a bit,' he said. 'We don't want to get too hot.'

So they moved a little further away to where a big boy was standing with his little brother beside him. Suddenly the big boy shouted something to a friend across the park. Then he bent and spoke to his brother. 'Now you be good, Fred,' he said sternly. 'I'll be back in a jiffy.' He ran off and disappeared behind the bonfire.

The little boy did nothing for a moment. But all at once a big tear, glistening in the firelight, rolled down his cheek and he slid a baby thumb into his mouth. Simon moved closer and patted his shoulder.

'It's all right, little Fred,' he said encouragingly, 'you can be with us till he comes back.'

Grandmother glanced down. Then she put out a big hand.

'Come and stand by me,' she said in a comforting kind of voice. 'They'll be letting the fireworks off soon.'

Without raising his eyes, and still sniffing, Fred shuffled across and took the hand.

'There we are,' said Grandmother.

'There we are,' said Simon happily. Then he said: 'Grandmother, I expect little Fred would like to hold a Sparkler.'

'Oh, would he?' said Grandmother, and got the Sparklers out.

But Fred only wanted to watch. So Simon held an extra

one for him. He waved his arms and jumped about, making big sparky circles in the air for as long as they lasted. Suddenly there was a whooosh! followed by a loud bang above their heads. Simon and Fred both jumped.

'Aha!' said Grandmother. 'Did you see that rocket?'

'It's all right, little Fred,' said Simon, moving round to take Grandmother's other hand, 'that was only a rocket.'

By now the bonfire was well alight, and at last the firework display really began.

'They're letting them off from the bandstand,' Grandmother remarked.

'They don't seem to be staying there,' said Simon, as a noisy jumping cracker suddenly leapt about, scattering the spectators. 'I expect little Fred isn't liking it very much,' he said.

But little Fred had stopped sniffing at last, and his eyes grew rounder and rounder as Silver Fountains, Roman Candles and showers of Golden Rain lit up the park. It was a wonderful sight. Sometimes, when there was a whizzing rocket or an extra loud bang, Simon leant across Grandmother.

'Hold on tight to her hand, little Fred,' he advised, 'then you won't be frightened.'

So they both did.

When the fireworks were nearly over, Grandmother opened the rest of the Sparklers and shared them out with the children near by.

Suddenly a gruff voice said: 'What did you want to move away for, Fred? I've been looking for you everywhere.'

So Simon and Grandmother said good-bye, and little Fred went off with his big brother.

On the way home, Simon talked about it all to Grandmother.

'I like fireworks,' he said.

'Good,' said Grandmother, 'so do I.'

'But,' said Simon, 'I expect anyone as small as little Fred must be quite frightened of them – sometimes.'

7 The attic

The frost had suddenly gone and the sun was shining, when Simon woke up one morning and heard two sounds.

The first was the quiet, familiar one of his Grandmother sleeping in her room next to his. The second was a dripping sort of sound, and it was coming from somewhere in the flat. Simon thought he'd see what it was. He tip-toed through to the sitting-room and looked about.

'Golly,' he said suddenly, and ran to wake Grandmother.

'It's me,' he said, as she sat up in bed with a start.

'What's up?' said Grandmother. 'You've got no shoes on.'

'You'd better come,' Simon said, 'there's water dripping from the ceiling in the other room, and it's getting wetter and wetter.'

'Eh?' Grandmother flung back the bedclothes.

It took her some time to find her feet inside her big white nightgown. She pushed them quickly into her bedroom boots and followed Simon into the sitting-room.

'Shiver my timbers!' she said in a surprised voice. 'The house has sprung a leak. We'd better have a bucket.'

Simon ran to fetch the yellow bucket from under the

kitchen sink. Soon the water was making a different sound as it went 'clunk, thunk', into the bucket.

'At least it can't escape now,' said Grandmother.

'We'd better see about it,' said Simon. Grandmother agreed. 'The sooner the better,' she said. 'First of all we'll get dressed, and then I'll telephone the plumber.'

Simon was just putting on his thick jersey when Grandmother came in. She was wearing two cardigans and a grey woolly muffler.

'Shivering shakes,' she said. 'The plumber can't come for ages. Everyone's got leaking houses, now the frost has gone.'

'Shivering shakes, we'll have a flood,' said Simon.

'I don't see why,' Grandmother tucked her muffler inside the two cardigans. 'We'll mend it ourselves. All we have to do is to get up into the attic.'

'How?' asked Simon.

'I've got some tall steps,' Grandmother said, 'but first we'll have some breakfast to keep the cold out.'

It was a long way up to the hole in the ceiling that led to Grandmother's attic. Simon helped her to open out the steps on the landing.

Then he looked up at the little trap-door that covered the hole.

'It's lucky you're not a short person,' he said.

Grandmother began to climb the steps.

'Stand well away,' she ordered. 'This is a very rickety contraption.'

Simon watched as she climbed carefully until she was near the top. Then she held on with her knees and used her hands to push open the trap-door above her head.

'There!' The door fell open with a bang and she grabbed the steps hastily. She drew a deep breath and spoke to Simon. 'So far so good,' she said happily.

Then Simon passed her the torch and two mopping-up cloths. Grandmother stretched and put these inside the attic.

'Are you coming up,' she said, 'or would you rather keep an eye on that bucket downstairs?'

Simon thought for a moment. 'I think I'd better come,' he said at last, 'in case you can't find something.'

So Grandmother helped him up the steps and pushed him through the ceiling into the attic.

'Golly!' he gasped as he landed on his front. 'I'd better light the torch, or you won't be able to see where you're coming to.'

Grandmother was already in the attic as far as her elbows, but the rest of her was standing on the top of the steps outside.

'Give me a heave,' she said. 'It's a bit of a tight fit.'

Simon pulled on the two cardigans. Grandmother gave a jump and a mighty push and shot forward into the attic.

'Hurray!' she panted. 'I'm here!'

At that moment there was a loud crash from the landing below. Nobody said anything. Then Simon looked out.

'It's a bit of a pity, Grandmother,' he said slowly. 'I see you've kicked the steps over.'

'There now,' Grandmother said calmly. 'I thought perhaps I had. Oh well, it can't be helped.' She picked up the torch and shone it around. 'First of all we'll see if we can find where all that water was coming from.'

Luckily there was a comfortable floor to walk on in the

attic, and Simon followed closely behind Grandmother as they searched for the leaking pipe.

'You've got a lot of things up here,' he said. He had just banged his leg on the corner of a suitcase.

'Aha!' said Grandmother suddenly.

She shone the torch on a narrow pipe which entered the attic near the roof. A large blob of water hung underneath it, and on the boards below a round, damp patch was getting bigger.

'We'll have this fixed in a jiffy,' said Grandmother. 'Pass me the cloths.'

Together they made a neat parcel of the pipe, winding the blob of water tightly inside it.

'There we are,' said Grandmother. 'That should do till the plumber arrives.'

'There we are,' agreed Simon. He gave the pipe a final pat. 'I wonder how the plumber will get *in*.'

'Oh,' Grandmother said, 'I'd forgotten about the steps. Let's have a look how far down it is.'

So Simon lay on the edge of the hole and looked at the landing below.

'*You're* a very good jumper,' he said.

But Grandmother wasn't listening. Instead she was rummaging about inside one of the boxes that were stacked in the attic.

'This ought to do.' She drew out a large white tablecloth with lacy edges. 'Come here, Simpey, I've had a good idea.'

Simon didn't say anything while Grandmother folded the tablecloth across his front, drew it under his arms, and tied it in a knot at the back. This still left two long ends for her to hold.

'Now – you've been in a swing – ' she began.

'Do you want to dangle me down?' he asked, rather loudly.

'It's all I can think of,' said Grandmother, 'and it's a very strong tablecloth.'

Simon looked at his feet. 'It would be the first bit,' he said, 'getting over the edge.'

'I know,' said Grandmother gently, 'but what else can we do?'

'All right,' said Simon.

He got down on the floor, with his legs dangling through the hole. Then he shut his eyes. Grandmother held the knot with one hand, and the tablecloth ends with the other.

'Slide out,' she said. 'I've got you in an iron grip.'

Simon wriggled himself over the edge, holding on with his hands till the very last moment. Then he was floating in the air with Grandmother hanging on behind. She began to let him down a little at a time. He opened his eyes.

'My word,' he said, 'it's like flying.' He felt the tablecloth as tight as a rope under his arms.

'All right below?' Grandmother sounded out of breath.

'All right,' said Simon, 'I'm nearly there.'

When his feet were only a little above the landing carpet, Simon shouted 'Let go!' and he jumped the last bit, being careful about not falling on the steps.

He pushed the tablecloth down himself and stepped out of it.

'Well done,' Grandmother said from above. She seemed to be taking off one of her cardigans.

'It was easy,' Simon said, 'and I know you've got very strong arms.'

At that moment the front-door bell sounded through the flat.

Simon ran and opened the door to the plumber.

' – And what's *your* trouble?' he said, stepping inside.

'We've mended the pipe, but my Grandmother's stuck in the attic,' said Simon.

'Well I never!' the man chuckled. 'Maybe we'd better rescue her.'

'Yes, and I practically flew down through the ceiling,' said Simon.

'Did you now?' said the plumber.

But Simon could see that he didn't really believe him.

8 The new neighbour

The weather was still quite cold, and Grandmother and Simon were having to stamp everywhere to keep their feet warm.

'Ta-rum, ta-rum, ta-rum,' Grandmother sang, as she whisked a duster about.

'Ta-rum, ta-rum, ta-rum,' echoed Simon, as he followed her with the carpet-sweeper.

'That should do,' said Grandmother at last. 'I think everything's tidy. Now we'd better go shopping.'

As they were leaving, Grandmother said suddenly:

'I forgot to tell you. Some new people are coming to live in the flat below.'

'How many, exactly?' asked Simon.

'I don't know yet,' Grandmother said. 'I think it will be rather nice to have some neighbours for a change.'

'I hope it will,' said Simon doubtfully.

'Well,' said Grandmother, 'we'll soon find out, for they're moving in tomorrow.'

The shopping did not take very long. Grandmother bought some sausages and some butter and a bag of liquorice allsorts. Then she went into the ironmonger's.

'I must get some clothes pegs,' she said. 'Mine are always vanishing.'

While she was buying the pegs, Simon noticed the piece of rope. It was tied up in a neat bundle, and was lying on the counter with a label on it: 'Sale Price 10p.'

'Have we got ten pence?' he asked Grandmother. 'It would be very handy to have all that rope.'

'Well – it would,' Grandmother agreed, 'but what should we do with it?'

'I could soon think of something when I got it home,' said Simon.

So Grandmother paid for it and the shopkeeper put everything into a paper bag. Simon tucked the bag under his arm and held it tightly all the way home. When they arrived, he took it straight in to the sitting-room and let the rope out of its bundle.

'Snakes alive!' said Grandmother, when she saw it. 'You've certainly got a bargain. There must be yards of it.'

'Snakes alive,' said Simon in a pleased voice, 'there's miles and miles and miles and *miles*.' He pulled the rope out in a long line, and it reached three times up and down the room.

Grandmother went to take her hat and coat off, and Simon sat on the floor and started thinking about the interesting things he could do with his rope. At last he had an idea, so he picked up one end of it and began.

Some time later, the flat was full of the sound of sizzling sausages, and Grandmother called to Simon from the kitchen.

'Come along,' she said, 'everything's ready. I hope you're as hungry as a hunter.'

There was a short silence. Then Simon's voice came from the sitting-room.

'I don't think I can,' he called. He sounded rather breathless.

Grandmother went through to see what was happening.

'Good gracious!' she exclaimed, peering round the door. 'You look just like a parcel!'

Simon was sitting on the carpet. He had had a busy time

tying himself up with the new rope and now there was hardly and inch of his legs to be seen. Round and round it went, and in and out of itself. There seemed to be a great many knots all over it. He was trying to undo one of them.

'I've been captured by the Indians,' he said gloomily. 'This is going to take a long time.'

'Dear me, what a pity,' said Grandmother, 'and all those lovely sausages getting cold.' She looked down at him thoughtfully. 'I don't suppose the Indians would want their prisoners to starve,' she said, 'so how about coming as you are?'

Simon began to look more cheerful. 'How about it,' he said, 'but you'll have to help me up.'

By the time he had finished eating, the prisoner was beginning to wriggle about uncomfortably.

'This rope is very knobbly underneath,' he said. 'Perhaps it would be a good idea if I was rescued now.'

'Perhaps it would,' agreed Grandmother, getting up. 'Let's have a look at those knots.' And she tackled them one by one.

That afternoon, Simon thought of several other ways to use his rope. It made a very good thing to jump over, when he tied one end of it to the table leg and the other to a chair. After that, he coiled it round and round on top of itself and then sat on it.

Later on Grandmother did some skipping with it, but she had to stop when the rope kept catching on the lamp-shade hanging from the ceiling.

'I don't want to go through the floor again, either,' she said.

Best of all, when he went to bed, Simon thought of tying one end of the rope to his door handle. He spent a long time pulling his door open and pushing it back, without having to get out of bed.

'This is a *very* handy thing,' he said.

The next morning, when Grandmother and Simon were

washing up the breakfast things, they both heard a heavy rumbling sound from outside.

'I'll go and look,' said Simon.

In a moment he was back in the kitchen. 'It's an enormous, gigantic van,' he said, 'and it's stopped outside our gate.'

'Really?' said Grandmother. 'I expect that'll be the furniture for the flat below.'

Simon began to have a very interesting time.

In between looking at his rope and helping Grandmother, he kept squinting out of the window to watch the furniture being trundled in below.

'They must be a very big family,' he remarked. 'They've got hundreds and hundreds of things.'

'I'll pop down in a little while, and see them,' Grandmother said. 'They might like some help, as it's their first day.'

When she got back, Simon had taken the new clothes pegs out of the bag and was busy counting them.

'Well – ' said Grandmother, 'I've seen our new neighbours.'

'I expect they're all in a terrible squash,' said Simon.

'No,' said Grandmother, 'they're not. And by the way,' she added casually, 'one of them is coming to tea.'

'Oh,' said Simon, 'which one?'

'She's a little girl,' said Grandmother, 'and her name is Prue.'

Simon looked up in astonishment.

'A little *girl*,' he said, 'oh goodness.' He picked up a clothes peg and stuck it on his jersey.

At about four o'clock there was a short ring on Grandmother's bell. Simon went to the door and opened it. A small girl stood there. She had long, straight brown hair. She was wearing a yellow cardigan and looked very tidy and neat.

'I've come to tea,' she said.

'I know,' said Simon, looking at her.

The little girl stared at him for a moment, gazing at the clothes pegs sticking out all over him.

'*You* look like a hedgehog,' she said.

'That's what I'm meant to be,' said Simon, looking pleased.

Then Grandmother appeared suddenly behind him and smiled down at the visitor.

'Hallo, Prue,' she said in her kind voice, 'we've been expecting you, come along in.'

While Grandmother finished getting the tea ready, Simon and Prue stood looking at each other. The little girl spoke suddenly, in her quiet voice.

'I would rather like to be a hedgehog as well,' she said. Simon thought for a moment.

'You can be half a hedgehog, if you like,' he said. He began taking off some of his clothes pegs. When Prue had stuck them carefully on to her yellow cardigan, they all sat down to tea.

'I hope hedgehogs like eating sandwiches,' said Grandmother, as she passed them round.

'Oh yes,' said Prue politely, 'they do.'

After tea they all sat round the fire. Everybody had a liquorice allsort, and Simon showed Prue his new rope.

'What a lot of it there is,' she said thoughtfully.

'I know,' said Simon, 'and we've done a lot of things with it.' He paused. 'It would be nice if we could think of something else,' he said.

'Well,' Prue said slowly, 'later on, you could let it down into the garden and I'll tie things on to it, like the bread or the milk or coal or something, and *you* could pull it up – ' she stopped for breath as Grandmother sneezed suddenly. ' – But just this minute, I don't mind being a horse, and you could make reins out of it, and we could gallop about a bit.'

Simon's eyes opened wide. He sat up and gave her a beaming smile.

'I think you're going to be a very nice person for me and my Grandmother to play with,' he said.

'Do you know,' said Grandmother chuckling, 'I think she is!'

9 Grandmother in trouble

Simon had just arrived to stay with his big kind Grandmother again. Her flat was the top half of a big house. It was lucky she had one little spare bedroom for him to sleep in.

Simon's mother had been the youngest of Grandmother's family of five, and although he was only six and Grandmother was seventy-seven, it never seemed to matter at all. Grandmother was full of exciting ideas and they both liked doing almost anything.

Simon was doing his unpacking when he heard Grandmother calling.

'Are you ready for tea, Simpey?' her hearty voice boomed through the flat.

'Yes, I am,' called Simon. He had a new football in a string bag and he took it with him into the kitchen.

'Welcome,' said Grandmother, smiling. 'I'm glad you're here again. I've been missing you a lot.'

Simon stood in the doorway and looked at everything. He smiled back and pushed his hair out of his eyes.

'I'm very glad I've come,' he said. Then he added, 'I expect we'll be able to have a little game of football soon.'

'Of course,' said Grandmother. 'We'll go to the park tomorrow. You need plenty of room with a football.'

So next morning, after breakfast, Simon shook his football out of its string bag. Then he went to find Grandmother. She was rattling about in her broom cupboard.

'I've just been getting my football ready,' he told her.

'Splendid!' Grandmother said. 'I shan't be long. I'm doing a little tidying up.'

'Oh,' said Simon. He moved over to the window and looked out. 'It would be a pity if it rained soon,' he said.

Just then, Grandmother pulled a long, strange-looking object from the cupboard and instantly several things came loose and clattered on to the floor.

'At the moment it's raining brooms and brushes,' she said. 'Come and help me put these back.'

'I've never seen that before,' said Simon, looking at the long pole Grandmother was holding.

'I know, I invented it myself last week,' Grandmother said proudly.

'It looks like a feather duster tied on to a broom handle,' said Simon.

'Exactly,' Grandmother said. She waggled the pole in the air. 'I used it for my spring-cleaning, to chase the cobwebs on the ceiling,' she explained.

'How did it reach them?' Simon looked at the pole thoughtfully. 'You've got quite long arms, but your ceilings are very high up.'

'I jumped it at them,' Grandmother said simply. 'Look, I'll show you.' She began leaping up and down the kitchen, whacking at the ceiling with the feathers on the end of the pole.

'There!' she said breathlessly, stopping at last. 'Can *you* see any cobwebs?'

'I expect I might if I was doing it,' said Simon, taking the pole.

So Grandmother flopped into a chair and watched while Simon did some jumping.

'Fine,' she said, after a while, 'I think that should do. Now we can get ready to go out.'

But as she took the pole from Simon, the end of it twirled round suddenly. It swept along the mantelpiece, caught the edge of a photograph in a silver frame and sent it crashing to the floor.

'Disaster!' cried Grandmother. 'There goes my young brother James!'

'Disaster,' said Simon. He peered at the photograph as Grandmother shook away the bits of broken glass. 'It's difficult to see your brother James,' he said. 'It's a very dark brown picture.'

'He's your great uncle,' Grandmother said. 'He went to live in Canada a long time ago.' She looked thoughtfully at Simon. 'The last time he came back was on his sixtieth birthday. *You* were born the year after that, so you just missed him.' She chuckled suddenly. 'What a pity. Your Great Uncle James is rather like a cracker. He's full of surprises.' She gave a small sigh. 'It seems a *very* long time since I saw him.'

At that moment, the doorbell rang. It was Prue, from the downstairs flat. 'Hallo,' she said to Simon. 'I saw you come yesterday.'

'Hallo,' said Simon. 'We've just broken Great Uncle James.' So Prue came in to look, and Grandmother swept up the bits of broken glass.

'We heard a lot of bumping on our ceiling,' Prue said. 'We wondered what it was.'

'It was us,' said Simon. 'We were springing and cleaning. Now we're going to the park to play football.' He looked at Prue. 'You could come and be a goalkeeper if you like,' he offered.

'I'll go and ask if I can,' Prue nodded.

'What a good idea,' Grandmother said thankfully; 'and I can sit on a seat and do the cheering.'

There was hardly anyone about when they reached the big piece of grass that people were allowed to play on in the park. The sun was shining and the air was crisp and fresh. Grandmother at once sat down on one of the wooden seats. 'Delicious!' she murmured. She closed her eyes and took several deep breaths. 'I'm just going to sniff in some of this beautiful spring air,' she said.

'We're not going to be a very big team,' Simon said loudly, looking at her.

Grandmother opened one eye. 'I'll wait till you've shown Prue how to play,' she said.

'I know how,' said Prue. She was trying to balance the football on her head.

'Well,' said Simon, 'perhaps you could come when you've finished your sniffing. We'll get the goalposts ready.'

He and Prue hurried about finding two sticks to make the goalposts. 'It's no good having any at the other end,' Prue said, 'because there won't be anyone there.'

They pushed the sticks in the ground in front of a tall, thick hedge which stretched across the end of the grass.

'When you miss one of my good shots, the hedge will catch it,' said Simon.

'Go on then,' said Prue, 'I'm ready.'

So they began the game. After a while, when Simon had scored three goals and Prue had saved the rest, Simon stopped running for a moment.

'We could ask Grandmother to be the goalkeeper now, if you like,' he said. 'Football is very warming-up when there's only one of you playing it.'

When they asked her, Grandmother agreed to come. She looked very big when she was standing between the goalposts, and at once she began dancing about with her hands in front of her, to be ready for the ball. Then Prue and Simon took it in turns to aim the ball at her. But Grandmother was a very good goalkeeper, and not a single shot went past her.

'It's very difficult to see where to kick it, when you keep hopping up and down,' Simon said, after a while.

'Yes,' agreed Prue, 'it is.'

'Put your toe *under* the ball,' Grandmother suggested. 'Wait a moment.' She strode across to Simon. 'I'll show you. Stand back, everyone!'

Simon and Prue waited while Grandmother placed the ball carefully on the grass. She walked back a little way and drew a deep breath. 'Now,' she said sternly, 'watch this!'

She took three big leaping steps towards the ball and kicked it so quickly that Simon and Prue never even saw her foot hit it. But they did see the football soar into the air like a rocket, whizz over the hedge behind the goal, and disappear. Almost at once they all heard the loud crackling, crashing, tinkling sound of breaking glass.

'Help,' said Prue softly.

'Oh dear,' said Grandmother.

'What a shot!' Simon beamed at her. Then he began to run. 'Come on!' he called. 'I expect you've broken something big this time.'

The ball had shattered two panes of glass in a large greenhouse which stood behind the hedge. It had gone straight through the roof and was lying just inside the door. An elderly park gardener stood looking at it. He was shaking his head, 'Children,' he said bitterly, as Prue and Simon arrived beside him. 'There's no peace with children.'

'It was a mighty shot,' said Simon. He stared up into the sky and remembered how it had looked.

'Now then,' the gardener spoke severely, 'which of you did it?'

Prue and Simpey looked at him.

'Hum – yes.' Grandmother's voice came from behind the gardener, making him turn sharply. 'I'm very sorry indeed,' she said earnestly, 'but when I kicked it I never meant it to go quite so far.'

The gardener's eyebrows practically disappeared over the top of his head.

'*You* kicked it?' He glared fiercely at her.

'I'm afraid so,' Grandmother nodded. 'I was showing the children how to do it, so it's all my fault, you see.'

'But it's *my* football,' Simon said quickly.

'– And none of your plants are hurt,' said Prue.

'Of course, I'll have to pay for the damage,' Grandmother said. 'You'd better have my name and address.'

'Huh,' muttered the gardener. He stared at Grandmother. 'Seems a funny story to me,' he said, wagging his head, 'a very funny story indeed.' He produced a pencil and began to take down particulars.

On the way home, nobody said very much, but when they reached the gate Prue's mother waved to them from a window. She was a small, quick, smiley person.

'Hallo!' she called. 'Had a good game?'

'Yes,' said Prue and Simon together.

'You're lucky,' Prue's mother said. '*I'm* starting my spring-cleaning today.'

When they'd said good-bye to Prue, Grandmother chuckled suddenly.

'Perhaps it's not such a bad day after all,' she said to Simon. 'I shall certainly have to have Great Uncle James repaired, and I've damaged a greenhouse, but at least my spring-cleaning is *quite* finished. I've not another thing to do.'

'Oh good.' Simon nodded heartily at Grandmother. 'So we'll be able to have another little game of football tomorrow.'

10 The bargain

One morning Grandmother gave Simon a large notice to fix on to her front gate.

'It's about the Church Sale today,' she said. 'We want as many people to go to it as possible. When you've finished, we'll look for some things to take.'

'I'll be back in a flash,' said Simon.

He stuck the notice on to the gate with seven pieces of sticky tape. Through the hedge he saw several people stopping to look at it. Then he ran back to help Grandmother.

'What sort of things are we taking?' he asked.

'Well,' said Grandmother, 'I've made a very fine fruit cake. But it would be nice if we could find one or two more things that other people might like to buy.'

'If other people are going to buy *our* things, I suppose we shall be buying theirs,' said Simon.

'That remains to be seen,' said Grandmother. She put a cardboard box in the middle of the sitting-room floor and placed the wrapped-up fruit cake inside it.

'Now,' she said, 'let's look about.'

After a while there were several more things in the box. There was a packet of plastic spoons, a tin of shrimps, and a new pair of bedsocks wrapped in flowery paper. Grandmother looked down at the collection.

'Well now,' she said, 'I wonder if that's enough?'

'Well now,' said Simon, 'I wonder if it is?' He took two books from a topply-looking pile on the floor and put them in the box.

'I expect they'll have enough books,' said Grandmother, taking them out again.

'It's a very difficult thing to fill a box when it keeps getting emptied,' Simon said.

But Grandmother was beginning to tidy up. 'Mrs Hunter is calling for us at two o'clock, and we ought to be ready,' she said.

So Simon started picking up the books. As the bookcase was full up already, he made a tall pile of them and put them against the wall beside it.

'Oh dear.' Grandmother looked at the pile. 'I wish I'd got some more bookshelves.'

'There's a lot of room in your best china tea-set cupboard,' said Simon, looking at it. 'The books would be very tidy in there.'

'But where could I put the china tea-set?' asked Grandmother.

'That could go in a very neat and handy little cupboard somewhere else,' said Simon.

'Alas,' Grandmother said, 'neat and handy little cupboards are very difficult to find. Gracious!' she exclaimed suddenly. 'The time's getting on. We'd better have something to eat.'

Mrs Hunter arrived promptly in a big blue car. She was a large, round, jolly person. She didn't come up to the front door of the flat, but blew her horn from the roadway and shouted through her car window.

'All ready? Good! Good!' She laughed and waved to Grandmother and then sat back with her fingers playing a little tune on the steering-wheel.

'Mrs Hunter's got a great enormous thing lying on the top of her car,' said Simon, looking at it through the window.

'Jumping snakes!' Grandmother exclaimed. 'So she has! I do believe it's a grandfather clock.'

'Jumping snakes, it's a very funny place to put it.' Simon began hurrying himself into his jacket.

'I expect she's taking it to the sale.' Grandmother opened the front door and began to go downstairs. 'I've gone,' she said, 'and I've got the box.'

So Simon slammed the front door and ran after her.

Grandmother got into the front of the car with her cardboard box. But before he entered the back, Simon looked up at the big clock which lay along the roof.

'It looks as if it's asleep,' he said. Then he climbed into the car.

Mrs Hunter nodded gaily at everyone. She said 'Good! Good!' twice more, started the engine and suddenly shot off at a great rate. Simon pressed his feet tightly against the seat in front of him.

'I expect we'll be there quite soon,' he said.

He was right. Mrs Hunter rushed the car round several corners, whizzed in front of a laundry van and drew up with a bang exactly outside the entrance to the Church Hall.

'There!' she said triumphantly.

'Thank you very much,' said Grandmother faintly.

'I hope the clock's all right,' Simon said.

Then they all got out. Mrs Hunter soon found several people to help with the grandfather clock. They undid some ropes and lifted it carefully off the top of the car. As it was carried inside the hall, Grandmother gave a little sigh.

'What a beautiful old clock,' she said. 'It would look very fine in my sitting-room. But I expect it will be much too expensive.'

'It would be very clangy in the night,' said Simon.

Grandmother looked more cheerful. 'I suppose it would,' she said. 'It might keep waking us up.' Then she looked at the things inside her cardboard box. 'Come along,' she said, 'we'd better deliver these before the sale starts.'

Inside the hall everything looked very gay and cheerful. Round the walls there were long tables covered with brightly coloured paper. Each table had been made to look like a little shop, and they all sold something different. Grandmother took her cake to the Home-made Cake Stall and then she and Simon went round the hall delivering the bedsocks, shrimps and plastic spoons.

'There's Mrs Hunter's clock,' Simon said suddenly.

'So it is.' Grandmother moved across to where it stood beside a table covered with coloured cushions.

The lady in charge of the stall was polishing the clock with a duster.

'It *is* nice, isn't it?' she said to Grandmother. 'Such a pity, though, I don't know whether we'll ever sell it. It hasn't got any works inside, you see, and nobody wants a clock that won't go, do they?'

'No *works*?' Grandmother looked astonished and disappointed.

'No, I'm afraid not,' said the lady. 'I understand they were lost during a removal.'

'I expect they fell out with a horrible clatter,' suggested Simon.

Grandmother didn't say anything for a moment. Then she put out a hand and stroked the warm brown wood.

'Poor old clock,' she said softly. 'Never mind, you've still got a very handsome face.'

There was a long narrow door down the front of the clock, and in the centre of this was a little round window. Simon pressed his nose against it.

'There's an empty nothing inside,' he said.

He wriggled his finger down the edge of the door and it suddenly came loose and swung open. 'My word,' he said, 'it's like a little cupboard.' He put his arm inside and waved his hand about. Then he looked at Grandmother. 'It's a very neat and handy little cupboard,' he said slowly. 'It would be a nice comfortable place for a china tea-set.'

Grandmother looked startled. She stared hard at the clock and became very thoughtful. At last she gently closed the narrow door and began to smile.

'The very thing,' she said, nodding. 'Of course, Simpey, the *very* thing. We could have some small shelves inside it, and the clock would still look beautiful in the sitting-room.'

' – And it wouldn't be clangy in the night,' agreed Simon.

'That settles it,' chuckled Grandmother. 'I wonder how much it is?'

The lady in charge of the stall said they could have the clock for only a pound. When Grandmother had paid her, she slapped a large red ticket on it, saying S O L D. Simon gave the clock a friendly bang. 'Now you belong to us,' he said.

As they left the stall, he and Grandmother turned round to have one more look at it.

'I've just thought,' said Simon.

'What?' said Grandmother.

'As *well* as being a china tea-set cupboard, our clock will be something else,' he said.

'Will it?' asked Grandmother.

Simon looked up at her. 'It'll be a sort of a Grandfather to go with a Grandmother,' he said. Grandmother nodded solemnly.

'Sort of,' she said.

11 The water picnic

Simon and his Grandmother had decided to have a water picnic because the weather was so hot.

They were sitting facing each other in a small rowing-boat on the big lake in the park, and Grandmother was pulling them along at a great rate. Tucked under a seat at the bottom of the boat were a paper bag full of sandwiches, a bottle of lemonade and two cardboard cups. The water made a slapping sound against the boat and from around the lake came the soft quacking murmur of the wild ducks.

'I expect rowing is quite easy,' said Simon. He watched Grandmother's strong arms going to and fro.

'Well, it is and it isn't,' said Grandmother. The brim of her sun hat flopped up and down and she was beginning to look rather hot.

'I think it would be a good idea for me to have a little row when you get tired,' Simon suggested.

'Be sure to keep a good look out,' said Grandmother. 'Don't forget I can't see behind me.'

'I am,' Simon said. He put his hands together to make a telescope and squinted down the tunnel he'd made with his fingers. 'There's a little island in the middle of the lake,' he said. 'We could go and visit it.'

'All right,' Grandmother agreed. She pulled away at the oars and began to sing in a happy, hearty sort of voice. 'Yo ho ho and a bottle of rum . . .'

'A bottle of what?' interrupted Simon.

'Rum,' puffed Grandmother. 'Pirates drink it when they're searching for treasure. It's good strong stuff.'

Simon looked interested. 'It would be a nice idea for us to be pirates,' he suggested. 'We could look for treasure on the island, and we've got the lemonade to drink.'

'So we have,' said Grandmother. 'A good thing too; this rowing is thirsty work.'

Simon sighed. 'I expect it'll be my turn soon,' he said.

'We'll change places when we reach land,' said Grandmother. 'We don't want to have a man overboard.'

So Simon began practising pulling his arms in and out until Grandmother said suddenly, 'Are we nearly there yet?'

'Oh, we just are,' he said in a hurry.

Grandmother barely had time to pull the oars in before there was a hefty bump. The boat rocked as it hit the grassy bank and Simon nearly toppled off his seat.

'The island arrived before I was ready,' he said.

'We're shipwrecked,' Grandmother said calmly. 'I don't think your telescope was working properly.'

'Yo ho *ho*,' Simon said. 'Can we change places now?'

All at once Grandmother noticed the packet of sandwiches which had rolled into the middle of the boat.

'The butter's coming through the bag,' she said. 'We'd better find a shady place to put our tea, or it'll melt away altogether.'

Simon looked at the island. 'If I got out, I could put everything in a cool little spot under those bushes,' he said.

'Right,' Grandmother agreed. 'But be quick, or the boat might sail off without you.'

She held on tightly to some feathery willow branches, and Simon hopped on to the island with the lemonade and sandwiches.

He was back in a moment.

'I wonder how I can get into your seat when you're sitting in it?' he said.

The boat rocked wildly several times before they each managed to get in to the right place. At last they were ready and Simon took hold of the oars.

'Everything's very wide apart,' he said. 'I'm having to do a lot of stretching.'

'Avast!' said Grandmother. 'Full steam ahead, everyone!'

Simon frowned deeply and pulled hard on the oars. 'Full steam ahead,' he said.

But the boat refused to go. Instead, the oars began dipping deeper and deeper into the water. This made the handles rise higher and higher, until Simon almost had to stand up to keep holding on to them.

'I wish they'd come out,' he said. He pulled until his face was scarlet.

Then suddenly they did.

The oars shot into the air, Simon sat down with a bump and Grandmother said, 'Help! Where's my lifebelt?'

There were large splashes of water all down the front of her dress.

'It's lucky it's a hot day,' she remarked, 'I expect I shall soon dry off.'

'It's funny how rowing is such a wetting thing to begin with,' said Simon.

'Very funny,' murmured Grandmother. 'You'd better try again.'

'It would be a good thing to use the telescope,' Simon said. 'I might go quite fast.'

So Grandmother looked through her fingers and Simon dipped the oars in again, this time trying to keep them just below the surface of the water. In and out they went, in and out, while sometimes the boat moved along and sometimes it didn't. Simon pulled and heaved, stood up, sat down, splashed water into the air, and often over Grandmother.

After a while Grandmother called out, 'Hard a-starboard!'

'How do you mean?' gasped Simon. He stopped rowing for a moment.

'I don't know what it *means*, exactly,' Grandmother said, 'but it has a good sea-faring sound.' She looked at Simon. 'Your face is bright red,' she said. 'Sit still and recover.'

So he did. Then he said, 'We haven't gone anywhere, and I've been rowing and *rowing*.'

'A very good thing,' Grandmother replied at once. 'Now it won't take long to row us back for tea.'

When they finally reached the island again, Simon drew a deep breath.

'I expect you'll be glad it's your turn to row us home,' he said.

Grandmother tied the little boat tightly to the willow tree. Then she stood up carefully and stepped on to the island.

'Keep close behind,' she ordered, 'and watch out for cannibals.'

So Simon followed until they reached the clump of bushes, where Grandmother pulled off her hat and sat down thankfully on the grass. Then she picked up the bottle of lemonade which was lying in the shade.

'You get the sandwiches,' she said to Simon, 'and I'll open the rum.'

Simon put his hand underneath the bushes. Then he knelt down and disappeared underneath them. He came out again and crawled right round them.

'Grandmother,' he said, at last, 'it's a very funny thing, but the sandwiches are not exactly here.'

'Jumping cuttlefish!' Grandmother exclaimed. She stopped pouring lemonade. 'Are you sure?'

'Yes, I am,' said Simon, 'and there's bits of paper bag all over the place.'

At that moment they both heard the noisy sound of ducks squabbling near by.

'Ho ho!' said Grandmother. 'Cannibals! Let's take a look.' Still sitting, she turned and gazed down the other side of the little island. 'Bless my soul!' she chuckled. 'So that's where our sandwiches have gone!'

'Oh goodness,' said Simon. He watched while a small party of brown ducks finished gobbling up the contents of the paper bag. 'It's not a very nice thing to eat other people's tea,' he said gloomily.

'Don't despair,' said Grandmother, 'we've still got the rum.' She handed Simon a brimming paper cup. 'In any case,' she added cheerfully, 'it's really too warm to eat anything.'

'Oh, is it?' Simon said. He took a big drink of lemonade and looked down at the ducks again. 'I suppose they get extra hungry with all that swimming about,' he said.

When they'd finished the lemonade, he began to look more cheerful.

'Yo ho ho, I think I'd better look for the treasure now,' he said.

'Well, I'll stay here and keep an eye on those ducks,' announced Grandmother, 'and I'll pick up half the bits of paper bag. You can collect the faraway pieces.'

'Oh help,' Simon said, and ran off.

When he returned a little later, he found Grandmother had gone back to the boat and was sitting in it.

'What ho, pirate!' she said cheerfully. 'Did you find anything?'

Simon shook his head. 'No,' he said, 'I didn't; there wasn't *anything* except ordinary stones and bits of wood and those old ducks.'

'Dear me,' said Grandmother, 'what a pity.'

'Yes,' said Simon. He began putting one leg into the boat, when Grandmother stopped him.

'Half a moment,' she said, 'I'm sure I've forgotten

something.' She suddenly clapped a hand on top of her head. 'My sun hat!' she exclaimed. 'I've left it beside the bushes!'

'I'll go and look.' Simon turned back. 'Maybe the ducks won't have eaten it yet.'

As Grandmother waited, she heard Simon give a loud excited shout. In a moment he dashed down the bank towards her. He was waving her sun hat in one hand, and holding up something shiny in the other.

'Grandmother,' he gasped hoarsely, 'I've found some treasure! Look! It's a fivepenny piece, and it was *exactly* beside your hat!'

'Shiver me timbers!' Grandmother looked hard at the coin, then gave it back to him. 'What luck,' she said, 'it's treasure all right. My word, it's very exciting being a pirate.' She put on her hat and got ready to begin rowing again.

'My word, it is,' agreed Simon. He climbed into the boat and began polishing the treasure on his shirt. 'I wonder if you can buy a real telescope for fivepence?' he remarked.

'We'll have to find out,' said Grandmother.

She pulled the boat along with swift, smooth strokes until they reached the landing stage on the edge of the lake. Then, as they walked home, Simon thought of something.

'It's funny that you didn't see the fivepence when you put your hat down on the grass,' he said.

'Yes,' said Grandmother, 'it is.' She smiled at Simon. 'But it's lucky *you* did,' she said.

12 A little gardening

'I was thinking of doing a little gardening,' said Grandmother one afternoon.

'Oh,' said Simon. 'I think I'm going to be very busy doing some sticking in.'

'I must look for the key to the garden shed,' Grandmother said thoughtfully. 'I expect some of the tools will need oiling.'

Simon looked interested.

'Have you got a squirting oil-can?' he inquired.

'Of course,' Grandmother said, 'a big one.'

Simon put down the pot of glue he was holding.

'I think I'd better come and help you,' he said. 'I expect some of your tools will be quite heavy to move.'

So Grandmother found the key of the toolshed and they

both went downstairs, and down the steps into the garden. This was divided into two halves. One piece belonged to the ground-floor flat and the other half, with the toolshed, belonged to Grandmother. She had a small lawn and two rose-beds, with a narrow stony path which ran round everything. Also, between the garden and the roadway, there was a dense green hedge which always needed cutting.

'Gracious me!' Grandmother exclaimed, as she looked at it. 'This hedge is covered in whiskers again! It's only a little while since I cut it.'

'The grass is very sprouty-looking too,' said Simon. 'You could have a hayfield if you left it.'

The key grated stiffly in the lock as Grandmother opened the garden shed.

'Oh dear,' she said ruefully, looking in, 'everything seems to be in rather a muddle.'

Simon squeezed between the lawnmower and an ancient deckchair and went inside. He sniffed loudly. 'There's a very interesting smell in here,' he said.

'You're right,' said Grandmother, 'there is.' She grasped the handle of the lawnmower. 'There's only one thing to do,' she said firmly. 'We must pull everything out and let some fresh air in.'

Simon held on to the deckchair as Grandmother rattled the lawnmower out on to the path.

'*That* sounds very clanky,' he said with satisfaction. 'It's going to need a lot of oiling.'

Then they both started to empty the shed. There were a great many garden tools. There was also an ancient bicycle which was taking up a lot of room at the back, and finally Grandmother handed out a greasy red can with a long spout.

'There's the oil-can,' she said. 'I think it's got some oil in it.'

Simon pressed the little lever down hard on the top of the can. A thick stream of greeny-yellow liquid spurted suddenly out of the end of it. He wiped his shoe on the grass.

'Yes,' he said, 'it has, quite a lot.'

'I shouldn't waste it,' Grandmother said mildly. She picked up a pair of garden shears, and opened and closed them stiffly, several times. 'You'd better begin with these,' she said, 'then I can make a start on the hedge.'

Simon gave the centre of the shears a hearty squirt.

'Whoops!' said Grandmother, stepping back. 'Just a few drops will do.' She tried the shears again and nodded. 'Splendid!' she said. 'I shall set to work at once.' She turned round and advanced towards the hedge, clicking the shears fiercely at it.

'Whoops,' said Simon, 'now I'll do the lawnmower.' He squirted oil into all the little holes he could find, and tried pushing the mower to and fro several times. 'You still sound rather clanky,' he said to it. 'I'd better wait till the oil goes in a bit.'

After that he decided to begin on the old bicycle. He oiled the wheels and the spokes. Then he did the pedals and the chain. He put a few drops of oil under the saddle, and on the place where the handlebars twisted in the middle.

'It's lucky the bell hasn't got a top on it,' he said, looking at it. 'I can give it a nice little oiling right inside.'

By the time he had finished, Grandmother had neatly clipped the whole of one side of the hedge. She came across the lawn.

'I'm about to sit down for a few moments,' she announced. 'How are you getting on?'

'Could you do the sitting on your bicycle?' asked Simon. 'I've been getting it ready for you.'

Grandmother looked at it doubtfully. She chuckled suddenly and put down the shears.

'I'll have a try,' she said. 'I wonder if it still fits me?'

Carefully she put a foot on one pedal and hoisted herself on to the saddle. Then off she went, wobbling along the path beside the lawn and round the two rose-beds, until she was approaching Simon again.

'Help!' she gasped. She pedalled swiftly past him. 'The brakes aren't working. How am I going to stop?'

She was on her way round the garden for a second time when Simon ran after her.

'Get ready to jump,' he called. 'I'm going to grab you!'

He raced to the front of the bicycle, and catching hold of one side of the handlebars, he held on with all his might.

'Leap for your life,' cried Grandmother. The bicycle stopped so suddenly that she lost her balance and they all tumbled sideways on to the grass.

Grandmother gazed at the sky for a moment.

'I'm glad it wasn't the rose-bed,' she said dreamily. Then she sat up slowly and looked at herself. 'You've certainly oiled the bicycle very well,' she remarked. She wiped a smear off one arm.

But Simon was watching the back wheel which was still spinning round gently all by itself. His face wore a pleased look.

'It isn't squeaking at *all*,' he said.

Grandmother got up stiffly from the grass.

'Oh dear,' she said, 'I think I am. I shall go and have a sit in the deckchair.'

Not long afterwards Prue and her mother emerged from the front door of the downstairs flat. Simon came out of the

toolshed and went across to show Prue the oil-can. Further down the garden, Grandmother was stretched out in the deckchair with her eyes shut.

'We're doing a little gardening,' Simon said.

'Very nice,' said Prue's mother. 'We're just going shopping.'

Simon gave the oil-can two big squirts to show Prue how it worked.

'I could stay and help you,' she said at once.

'Oh no, you couldn't,' said her mother firmly. She

looked at the oil on Simon's trousers. 'I shall need you to help me carry things.'

'I don't expect we'll be long,' Prue said hopefully. She followed her mother through the small iron gate and left it to clang noisily behind her.

'I'd quite forgotten about that gate,' said Simon, when they'd gone. He examined its rusty hinges and lifted the oil-can. 'This will want a lot of extra oil, because people are going in and out of it all the time,' he said.

When he'd finished squirting all the rusty bits of the gate, there was still some oil left in the can. Simon looked down the front of himself.

'I expect I shall be needing to have a little wash soon,' he said thoughtfully. He saw that Grandmother still seemed to be very comfortable in her deckchair. Then he gave the oil-can a little shake and started walking towards the house. 'But it would be a pity not to use this all up first,' he decided. He ran up the steps and disappeared inside.

When he came out again, Grandmother was busy putting the tools back in the garden shed.

'I've a feeling it's time for tea,' she said firmly. 'I shall finish the hedge tomorrow.'

'Here's the oil-can,' said Simon. He handed it in. 'It's empty.'

'How surprising,' said Grandmother, raising her eyebrows.

She shut the shed door and locked it. This time the key swung easily, and a little oil trickled out of the keyhole.

'*That's* better.' Grandmother held the key carefully in two fingers. 'I see you've been busy.'

'I have.' Simon was on his way towards the house. 'But wait till you see the kitchen,' he said. 'I've oiled *everything* for you.'

'My goodness,' said Grandmother, 'have you?' She began to hurry after him.

'My goodness, I have,' Simon said, 'and it took ages and ages.'

They couldn't have tea till Grandmother had found a big cloth and had done a lot of wiping-up.

'It wasn't so drippy when I left it.' Simon looked at the trickles of oil running down the door.

'That's why you only need a little,' said Grandmother, wiping the cold tap before she filled the kettle. She also wiped the light switches and the drawer handles, and then she rubbed over the chair seats before they sat down. 'Oil takes you by surprise,' she said.

Simon smiled suddenly. 'I forgot to tell you,' he said. 'I've oiled the front gate all over. I expect Prue and her mother will be taken by surprise when they get home.'

'What!' exclaimed Grandmother.

'I *like* gardening,' said Simon. 'I'll help you again tomorrow.'

13 At the sea

Simon would soon be going home. But on the last day of his visit Grandmother had a specially good idea.

'It's going to be fine,' she said. 'We could go to the sea in a bus and take our lunch and tea with us.'

Simon rolled the very last cornflake round the end of his tongue until it melted suddenly and was gone.

'How do you know?' he asked.

'Know what?' Grandmother began clearing the breakfast table.

'That it's going to be a fine day,' said Simon.

'Because of the daisies,' Grandmother said. 'Look down on the lawn, they're all opening up, so as not to miss it.'

Simon climbed on to the window seat and looked outside. Three daisies sat in the middle of the tiny lawn in the garden below. Their faces were turned up towards the sky.

'*I* think they're watching for aeroplanes,' Simon said, 'but I'd like to go to the sea.'

'We'd better hurry, then.' Grandmother gathered the last of the dishes on to the tray. 'It's your turn to dry,' she said. 'Then we'll get ready.'

Simon wished he'd got six more pockets in his trousers. He had so many things he wanted to take with him. In the end he managed to squeeze in a short piece of rope, a packet of paper flags on sticks, three bits of yellow chalk, a canvas bag to collect interesting stones in, and half a bar of chocolate. He tucked his digging spade under his arm.

Grandmother was putting their lunch and tea into her big red hold-all. She looked at Simon.

'You seem to be a very funny shape,' she remarked.

Simon patted his bulgy pockets. 'I'll take it all out when we get there,' he said.

'Now then,' Grandmother looked thoughtful. 'I think that's everything. Your bathing trunks – my sun hat – front-door key and money. Yes.' She swung the red hold-all round in a happy circle and smiled down on Simon. 'Right!' she said. 'Then off we go!'

It was not very far to the sea from Grandmother's flat, but the bus was full to bursting. Simon had to sit on top of the hold-all on top of Grandmother. He had a very good view of everything.

'What ho!' Grandmother said, after a while. 'It certainly is hot. I hope the sandwiches are not too squashed.'

'What ho, my chocolate is,' said Simon.

They were both glad when they got on to the sandy

beach at last. At the foot of the rocky cliffs they found a shady little corner to put their things in. Grandmother spread out the big towel and put the hold-all down beside it. Simon began to undo his pockets. The chocolate was still in the packet, but it wouldn't sit up straight.

'I think it would be better if I ate it now,' he suggested.

'So do I,' Grandmother agreed. Then she began searching about in the hold-all.

'Here we are,' she said at last. She pulled out a long piece of string with a whistle tied to the end of it.

Simon watched as she made a knot in the string and hung it round her neck.

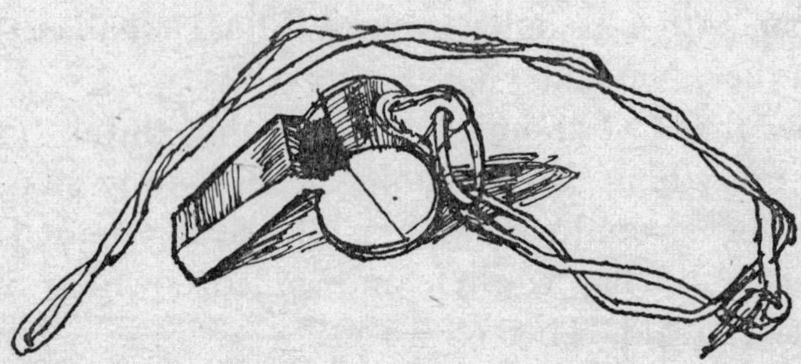

'I didn't know you'd got that,' he said.

'Watch out,' said Grandmother, 'I'm going to blow a mighty blast.' She put the whistle in her mouth and drew a deep breath.

Simon took a deep breath too, but it came out again with a rush when he heard the noise that the whistle made. A shrill whee-ee-ee echoed all over the beach. The sound seemed to be everywhere. Even when Grandmother stopped blowing, Simon thought he could still hear a faint ee-ee-ee coming from the top of the cliffs.

'Golly,' he said faintly, 'that was fine. Like a train.' Then he added, 'Those people are looking at us.'

'Yes – well.' Grandmother let the whistle hang down again and pulled Simon's bathing trunks out of the hold-all. 'I brought it in case I lost you on the beach. I can't go shouting all over the place. Be sure to come if you hear it again.'

Simon didn't say anything much till they were walking down towards the water. The whistle bumped about on Grandmother and sparkled in the sun.

'I was thinking,' he began, 'wouldn't it be better if I had it?' He pushed a bit of golden hair out of one eye. 'Then every time I get lost I can blow it, and you'll know where I am.'

Grandmother settled her big floppy sun hat firmly on her head, and gathered her skirts a little, ready for paddling.

'I'll tell you what,' she decided, 'we'll share it. I'll have it until after lunch, then *you* can have it till tea-time. That way neither of us can get lost.'

Simon stretched his arms out wide and ran like the wind towards the sea.

After lunch, Grandmother sat underneath her hat, keeping the sun out of her eyes. Simon had the whistle round his neck, and he began to dig a hole in the sand. But every time he bent down the string kept catching on the handle of his spade.

'Bother!' he said, and stopped digging.

It was then he saw the grey and white bird watching him from the rocks above his head. Its curvy beak kept opening and shutting, as if it might be feeling hungry. Simon put his spade down carefully. He took a paper bag of sandwiches from the top of the hold-all. Then he walked towards the cliff.

He had climbed quite a long way up it when he suddenly wondered if sea-gulls really liked banana sandwiches. All at once his left foot slipped and he stayed quite still. A piece of rock was trying to push itself into his forehead.

'*I'm* not lost, but I expect the sea-gull is,' he said to no one in particular. 'I think I'd better blow the whistle.'

It took him some time to get it into his mouth because of his face being so squashed against the cliff. It was rather a

squeaky blow, too, but Grandmother had very good ears.

'Ahoy there!' Almost at once her cheerful voice called up. 'You might have waited for me, Simpey!'

Simon gulped. 'I'm waiting now,' he said loudly.

He heard scrapy scrambling noises coming from beneath him. There was a tearing sound.

'Oh, well,' Grandmother's voice was a lot nearer, 'it's only an old skirt anyway.'

Suddenly Simon found he didn't seem to be squashed up against the rock any more. He heard Grandmother puffing loudly, and looked down. Her face was just beside his shoe. 'Are we going up any further, or what?' she asked.

'There was a lost sea-gull,' Simon said. 'That's why I blew the whistle.'

'Quite right.' Grandmother was still puffing. 'It's been found now, at any rate.'

'Is it time for tea yet?' asked Simon.

'Exactly time,' said Grandmother. 'Let's go down.'

And they did.

They had just finished the lemonade when Grandmother picked up the little canvas bag Simon had brought with him.

'What about this?' she said. 'We've never collected any stones yet.'

'I know,' said Simon. 'Let's begin now.'

So they both collected stones until it was time to catch the bus.

14 It's magic!

After Christmas Simon was visiting Grandmother again. The weather had been growing colder and colder, and Grandmother's coalshed had been empty for some time. Then, one morning, there was a sharp frost.

'We shall turn into icicles if we don't get some coal soon,' said Grandmother. She put on two cardigans and turned on the electric fire.

Simon decided to wear his new dressing-gown on top of his clothes. Grandmother had made it for him out of a blanket she had bought at the Sales, and it was all colours of the rainbow.

'It's a good thing this is a bit big,' Simon said. He pulled the collar up over his head and face, and pushed his hands deep into the large pockets.

'Goodness! Where have you gone to?' inquired Grandmother.

Simon's voice came out of the dressing-gown.

'I think I'm going to stay in here till I'm a little bit warmer,' he said.

He was still wearing it when Prue arrived from the downstairs flat.

'Are you going to bed?' she asked him.

'No, I'm not,' said Simon. 'I'm keeping warm till we get some coal.'

'That's a nice fluffy dressing-gown,' remarked Prue.

'I know,' Simon said, it's a Christmas present from Grandmother.'

'*I* got a book about magic for Christmas,' said Prue. 'It tells you how to do spells and things.'

Simon looked at her. 'Come on then,' he said, 'let's do some.'

'While you're at it,' Grandmother remarked, 'you can magic me some coal from somewhere. That would be very useful.'

'I don't think it said anything about coal in the book,' said Prue.

'Well, what *did* it say then?' Simon asked.

'There was a lot about Aladdin and his lamp.' Prue said. 'He kept rubbing it and then magic things kept happening.'

'All right,' said Simon, 'we could try that. Let's rub everything.' He took off his dressing-gown. 'I'm beginning,' he added.

He got down on the floor and began rubbing the table legs as hard as he could. Prue began with the coal-scuttle, and between them they rubbed everything they could think of. They rubbed the carpet, the chairs and the book-case. Then they rubbed the windows, the pictures and the door knob. They crawled beneath the frilly curtain in front of the window seat, rubbing as they went. When they came out, Simon stood up.

'I think I'd like to do something else,' he said.

'So would I,' agreed Prue. 'Let's go in the kitchen and find some things to make a spell with.'

Grandmother poured out cocoa for everybody while Prue and Simon were making their spell. They mixed up salt, flour and mustard powder in a bowl. Simon added a pinch of nutmeg and some vinegar and water. Then they stirred them all together and waited for something to happen.

'Have your cocoa,' said Grandmother, after a while.

'I wish magic wasn't so difficult,' Simon said gloomily.

'What you really need are some magic words,' advised Grandmother, 'but you have to be sure to choose the right ones.' She waved her cocoa spoon over the bowl. 'Abracadabra,' she said solemnly, 'salt fish and herring bones.'

'Abracadabra,' echoed Simon, 'jellyfish and seaweed . . .'

' – And fairy frogs and knitting needles,' Prue added hopefully.

But still nothing happened.

'Never mind,' said Grandmother, 'perhaps we'll be luckier next time. But I've just had a good idea.' She smiled at them both. 'There's an old deserted garden near here. It's full of trees, almost like a real wood. We could collect some stuff to burn on the fire, and we might find something interesting.'

Simon and Prue looked at each other and nodded.

'We'll go as soon as we've cleared up,' said Grandmother.

Before setting off, Grandmother frowned thoughtfully. 'We shall need something fairly big to bring the firewood back in,' she said.

'It would be nice if we had a little cart,' said Simon, 'with a pony to pull it.'

'It would be nice if we had a magic wand,' Prue said, 'then we could have *anything*.'

'I know!' exclaimed Grandmother suddenly. 'We'll take the wheelbarrow. That should do splendidly.'

The wooden wheelbarrow lived in a corner of the garden. It was big and rattly, and there was just room to get it through the front gate. Grandmother was the only person big enough to push it, so Simon said he would push her and Prue said she would push him, and they were soon going along at a great rate.

'Everybody's looking out of their windows,' Simon said, while they waited to cross the road. 'I expect they think it's a train.'

'It's a good thing we haven't far to go,' said Grandmother.

They pushed the barrow up a narrow lane and then entered an old tumbledown gateway. The house that had belonged to the garden had gone, but a great many big fir trees still remained, huddled closely together. It was a lonely, gloomy place.

'Whoa!' said Grandmother. 'The barrow's stuck. I think we'd better leave it here.' She banged her hands together. 'Shivering shakes! Hurry up everyone, we want plenty of wood. I'm looking forward to a nice fire as soon as we get home.'

'Shivering shakes!' Simon had run on ahead. 'I expect I shall collect fifty fir-cones.'

'So shall I,' called Prue. 'I've seen two already.'

It wasn't long before the wheelbarrow began to look quite full. There were lots of dry twigs beneath the trees, and fir-cones seemed to be everywhere. Simon and Prue also discovered an ancient bird's nest and a blue coat button. But it was Grandmother who found the feather. They were in the darkest part of the wood when she picked it up.

'Tu-whit tu-whoo,' she said in a mysterious voice. 'Look what I've found.'

The little feather was brown and soft-looking, and lay curled up on her big hand.

'It's a very nice little thing,' said Simon kindly. 'Why were you too-whooing?'

'Well,' Grandmother said, 'I'm almost sure that this is an owl's feather. It's the right sort of place to find it.'

Prue looked up into the fir tree. 'I expect he sits up there at night,' she suggested.

'I can put it in my pocket if you want to collect it,' Simon offered.

'All right.' Grandmother gave it to him. 'It would be nice to keep it,' she said, 'for an owl is a strange, magical kind of a bird.'

'*Magical?*' breathed Prue. She lowered her voice to a whisper. 'Perhaps we could do a real spell with the feather,' she said.

'It isn't any good,' objected Simon. 'We don't know the proper words.'

'But the feather would do the magic,' Prue said earnestly. 'We can just make something up.'

'Ah,' Grandmother interrupted mildly. She considered them both. 'It's high time we were starting back,' she said. Then she glanced at Prue and added hastily, 'but we could do it once more, all together, very quickly.'

'What shall we wish for?' Prue said at once.

'A nice sack of coal.' Grandmother stamped her feet up and down. 'I'm getting very chilly.'

'Let's wish for a coal-*mine*.' Simon giggled. 'Then if it comes, we'll all fall in.'

So they began. Grandmother took the feather first and waved it in the air. Then she shut her eyes.

'Abracadabra,' she muttered, 'snakes' eyes, spider's legs, buttered toast and tea.' She passed the feather to Prue.

'Abracadabra,' Prue said softly, 'goldfish, skipping ropes, lollipops and chocolate. There!' Simon took the feather.

'Abracadabra, tu-whit tu-whoo, birds' nests and buttons,' he said, all in one breath.

It was quiet in the wood and everybody stayed quite still.

'Alas!' said Grandmother at last. She smiled kindly at Prue. 'Magic is a strange thing,' she said, 'but don't be too disappointed, it *could* happen when you're not expecting it.' She lifted the wheelbarrow. 'All hands to the pump!' she called out cheerfully. 'I need a little help!'

'All hands to the pump.' Simon tugged at the front wheel till it came out of the leaves. 'You can borrow our feather when you want to,' he told Prue. Then they set off.

They were all very tired when they reached the front

gate once more. Simon ran to hold it open for Grandmother.

'My feet are crunching on something,' he said, as she went past him.

Then Grandmother's feet began crunching, and so did Prue's.

'Jumping beanstalks!' Grandmother put the barrow down and pointed. 'Look there!'

All along the path was an uneven trail of small black lumps. They led to the coal-house door. In two strides Grandmother reached the door and pulled it open. The little shed was nearly half full of beautiful, shining black coal.

'Gracious stars,' she chuckled, '*that's* a bit of luck!'

Prue drew a deep breath and smiled. 'No, it isn't,' she said, 'it's magic. I *thought* it would work.'

'Jumping beanstalks,' Simon said slowly, 'it must have been that feather.' He drew it out of his pocket and looked at it. 'You're a very clever little thing,' he said. Then he look at Prue and Grandmother.

'I wonder *which* of us knew the right words?' he said.

15 The sledge

The snow had been falling softly and steadily all through the night. Now, in Grandmother's garden, it was nearly seven inches deep, and Simon was playing in it. He had been trying to make a snow model of a sledge, and was busy sitting on it when the milkman arrived.

'Hallo!' he called out to Simon as he passed. 'Off to the North Pole, are you?'

'I'm not off anywhere,' Simon said, getting up, 'but I would be if it was a real sledge.' He jumped about a bit to get himself warm.

The milkman looked surprised.

'Haven't you got one, then?' he asked.

Simon shook his head.

'Well now,' said the milkman thoughtfully, 'it so happens that *I've* got an old sledge at home. My children had it, but they're all grown-up now.'

'Oh,' said Simon, 'I expect they liked having it.'

'It's a bit shabby, but it's good and strong,' said the milkman. 'How about you borrowing it while the snow's here?'

Simon stayed quite still for a moment. Then he took the milkman's hand.

'Could you come and see my Grandmother at once?' he said.

So the milkman and Simon and Grandmother all had a cup of cocoa together and said what a good idea it was for Simon to have the sledge.

That afternoon the sledge arrived. The milkman brought it as he had promised, and he had kindly put a new piece of rope on it, to pull it along with. When he had gone, Grandmother walked round it. 'That's a fine sledge,' she said, 'and strong enough for an elephant. We must try it at once.'

'I can be ready in a flash,' said Simon, going for his coat.

'I won't be long,' promised Grandmother.

So they both rushed about getting ready. Grandmother put on some new Wellington boots she had just bought, and Simon wore a cosy red hood she had knitted for him. They both seemed to have on a great many clothes.

'I feel very bulgy,' said Simon, when at last they went outside.

Grandmother gave him half of the sledge rope to hold.

'Heave ho, my hearties,' she said, as they set off.

'Heave ho,' said Simon. 'Can we go to the North Pole?'

'I don't think so,' Grandmother said, 'it's rather far for now. But we'll go to the common. It's a very good place for sledging.'

It was hard work trudging through the snow and they were both glad when at last they arrived. There were lots of other people with sledges, and most of them were going to the far end of the common where the ground sloped down steeply for quite a long way.

'What a very slidy-looking place,' Simon said, as they reached it.

'We needn't go too fast to begin with,' said Grandmother.

She tied her woolly scarf more tightly under her chin, and tucked the ends inside her coat collar. 'Now,' she said, 'are you ready?'

'I suppose I am,' said Simon.

'This sledge seems very near the ground,' Grandmother remarked. She bent herself carefully and sat on it with a heavy thump. 'There!' She smiled encouragingly at Simon. 'You get on behind me and hold tight,' she said.

There was just room for them both on the sledge. Grandmother's shiny boots stuck out on either side, and Simon stretched his out, too, as far as they would go. Then Grandmother took hold of the rope and settled herself comfortably.

'Watch out!' she said, digging her heels in. 'We're off!'

As the sledge tipped on to the slope, it gathered speed and Simon lifted his legs off the ground so as not to stop it. He clutched as much of Grandmother as he could and pressed his cheek into her back. The snowy ground began to slip by faster and faster, and as Simon felt the wind on his face, he began to wonder if he was about to fall off.

'Grandmother,' he gasped, 'I'm finding it very slippery on here!'

There was a sudden spray of snow and the sledge began to slow up rather bumpily. Grandmother was digging her heels hard into the ground.

'Hold on!' she shouted. 'I'm going to stop!'

As they slowly drew to a standstill, Simon slid gently off into a heap of soft snow.

'That was very clever of you,' he said. 'I didn't think you could.'

Grandmother's eyes were sparkling. 'Come on,' she said, turning round and starting off up the slope, 'we'll do it again. You push the sledge up from behind.'

When they reached the top, they both got on to the sledge and began once more. This time Simon didn't feel so much that he was falling off and they travelled a little further down the hill. They climbed up to the top and did it again; then again and again, until Simon's nose and cheeks were nearly the colour of his hood. At the top of the hill once more, he said to Grandmother, 'I'm enjoying the sledging. It's a pity all this pulling up is very tiring.'

'Look here,' said Grandmother suddenly, 'how about

my having a turn by myself? You can wait here and try and guess how far I'll get.'

'By yourself?' Simon looked down the hill. 'Golly.'

Grandmother thumped herself firmly on to the sledge. 'Can you see that bush?' She pointed far down the slope. 'I'll see if I can manage to reach that.'

'Golly,' said Simon again. 'I expect you'll fall off with me not being there behind you.'

'Nonsense!' said Grandmother cheerfully. She gripped the rope. 'Now,' she said, 'give me a push.'

So Simon did, and off she went, careering down the slope. He heard her say gee-up! and at first she began waving her arms up and down and urging the sledge forward as if it was a horse. But Grandmother was quite a heavy person, and soon the sledge was travelling very fast indeed. On and on it sped, until it started giving little leaps and jumps over the rough bits.

'Whizz!' said Simon, banging his hands together. 'Whizz! She's nearly at the bush!'

Grandmother wasn't waving her arms any more. She was leaning back and seemed to be pulling hard on the rope.

'Coo!' said a voice next to Simon. 'Just look at that old lady! Where does she think she's going to, the North Pole?'

At that moment Simon saw Grandmother dig her left foot into the snow. The sledge tilted up, curved round in a big half circle, and with Grandmother still clinging on, shot round the bush and went clean out of sight.

'Heave *ho*,' said Simon, and charged down the hill to the

rescue. When he found Grandmother, she was sitting on the sledge polishing her boots with a handkerchief.

'Hallo,' she said calmly, 'I've been waiting for you.'

Simon couldn't speak for a moment because he was puffing out loud. Then he said, 'I thought you'd fallen off.'

'Goodness,' Grandmother looked surprised, 'did you really?'

'It's funny how the back of your coat is all covered with snow,' said Simon as he helped her up.

'It's very blowy stuff,' said Grandmother.

The next morning, the milkman found Simon polishing the sledge.

'Well?' he inquired. 'How did you get on yesterday? Did you get to the North Pole?'

'No,' said Simon, 'but I think Grandmother did.'

16 The biggest surprise of all

On a cold, snowy morning, Grandmother got up to find a letter waiting on the mat.

'Three cheers!' she said, when she saw it. 'It's from my brother James, in Canada.'

'You mean my Great Uncle James in the dark brown photograph?' asked Simon.

Grandmother nodded and opened the envelope. 'I wish he'd send his letters by airmail,' she remarked; 'they're always such a long time coming.' She put on her spectacles. 'Now,' she said, 'we'll find out what he's been up to.'

Simon waited while Grandmother read the letter. Halfway through it her eyebrows rose in surprise.

'Good gracious!' she muttered. Then she began to smile as she hurried on to the end. When she'd finished it, she took off her spectacles and stared at Simon. 'I don't believe it!' she exclaimed.

'My goodness,' Simon said, 'what *has* he been up to?'

'He's coming back to England,' Grandmother said simply. 'And not only that,' her eyes sparkled, 'he's coming for good, to live here!'

Simon looked interested. 'I remember you said he was

always full of surprises,' he remarked. 'I wonder when he'll get here?'

'He doesn't say exactly.' Grandmother examined the letter again. 'Not for some time, I suppose. He'll have a lot to do before he leaves.'

'Oh, goodness,' Simon frowned, 'it would be a pity if I'd gone home first.'

But Great Uncle James surprised them both.

Two mornings later, they were finishing breakfast, when there was a loud bang in the street outside. Then they heard a car door slam, and before Simon had time to reach the sitting-room window they heard someone mounting the steps to the front door. Suddenly the doorbell rang. Immediately afterwards a deep voice boomed, 'Ahoy there! Anyone at home?'

At once Grandmother pushed back her chair.

'Ahoy!' she shouted gaily. She beamed at Simon. 'I'd know that voice anywhere!' she said. 'Come along,' she smiled happily, 'it's high time you met your Great Uncle James!'

Simon had never seen anyone so big in all his life. Great Uncle James was wearing a huge, flappy, leather coat with an enormous yellow woollen muffler, and he brought a great blast of cold air with him into the flat.

'Kate!' He gave Grandmother a mighty hug, then swung her round in a circle as easily as if she had been a fairy.

'It's nice to see you, James,' she said calmly, when he had put her down again. 'We didn't expect you quite so soon.'

'Came by air,' said Great Uncle James. Then his vivid blue eyes stared down at Simon. 'Hallo, boy,' he said, in his deep-down voice.

'Hallo, Great Uncle James,' Simon said. 'We heard a loud bang. Have you got a puncture?'

The blue eyes looked surprised.

'Certainly not. That's the car. Always bangs. Quite all right.' Great Uncle James was no chatterer. 'Got a lot of stuff to unload, though. Want to come and help?'

'Here's your coat,' said Grandmother.

So Simon hastily pulled it on while Grandmother made for the kitchen.

'I'd better get some more breakfast ready,' she suggested.

'Good idea!' Great Uncle James agreed heartily. 'I could eat a dozen eggs!'

'A dozen eggs,' Simon repeated under his breath as he went out. 'Golly!'

Great Uncle James' car was standing in the snow. It was a remarkable sight. It was big and old-fashioned. It had no hood on it, and was painted bright yellow. Except for the driving-seat, every corner of it seemed to be full of suitcases, boxes and parcels. There was one immensely long thick package covered in brown paper. It lay on top of everything else and stuck out over the back of the car. It looked exactly like a wrapped-up lamp-post.

Simon gave a broad smile as he looked at everything.

'You've got a nice lot of things,' he said. 'What shall we take out first?'

Great Uncle James gave him two cardboard boxes to carry upstairs, and began heaving his suitcases out of the car. Before long, there was hardly room to move in the little hall.

'Jumping Jackdaws!' Grandmother stood in the kitchen doorway and surveyed the growing pile of luggage. 'Is there much more?' she inquired. 'I hope we shall get the front door shut.'

'It's just about to be the last thing,' Simon told her, 'and you'll be quite surprised when you see it.'

At that moment the front end of the long brown-paper

parcel entered the flat. Great Uncle James was somewhere at the other end of it.

'Here you are, Kate!' he shouted from outside. 'I brought you a little present. Where do you want it to go?'

'A present?' Grandmother said faintly.

She watched as more and more of the parcel appeared, until Simon had to guide it half-way into the sitting-room. Finally, Great Uncle James brought his end inside and laid it on the carpet.

'Good!' he said. 'That's the lot. How about that breakfast?'

He only ate three eggs after all, for Grandmother hadn't any more.

'We'll go out and stock up later,' she said.

'I expect you're wondering what's in your parcel,' Simon suggested. He had been hopping in and out of the kitchen looking at it.

'I can hardly wait,' Grandmother declared.

So Great Uncle James took a large penknife from his pocket and went through to undo Grandmother's present. He had the paper off in no time, and then stepped back to let them see. Before them lay a huge block of wood, nearly as big as a tree-trunk, and painted from head to foot in bright, glaring colour. It was covered in carvings of strange-looking animals, curious faces, and weird shapes of every kind.

'Well?' Great Uncle James smiled proudly.

'*Well!*' Grandmother gazed at it, speechless.

'My word,' said Simon. He touched it with his toe. 'What exactly *is* it?'

'An Indian totem pole,' said Great Uncle James. 'Most

American Indian tribes have 'em. Sort of a family tree. Like putting your name up outside the front door.'

Suddenly Grandmother flopped down into a chair and began to laugh and laugh.

'James,' she said, 'there's nobody like you. What a splendid present. I think it's the biggest one I've ever had.'

Simon and Great Uncle James both looked very pleased.

'It would be a nice little idea to put it outside *your* front door,' Simon suggested to Grandmother.

'Just for the moment I can't think where we're going to put anything,' Grandmother said, looking round.

'No,' Great Uncle James agreed helplessly, 'nor can I.'

It was decided that Simon would sleep on a camp-bed, while the visitor borrowed his bedroom.

'Hope you don't mind, boy,' said his great uncle.

'I'd *rather* sleep on a camp-bed,' Simon said, 'but I expect your feet will stick out of mine.'

And so they did. In fact, after only one night, Great Uncle James seemed to be too big for the flat altogether. Most of his luggage had to stay in the hall, and the more he unpacked, the fuller everywhere seemed to become. Some strange things appeared from his luggage. A red flannel dressing-gown, the size of a tent, and a shoe-horn three feet long. He gave Simon a tin of maple syrup and then a pair of real snow shoes. Simon put these on at once.

'They'll be very handy when I'm used to them,' he told Grandmother, 'but they're rather trippy at the moment.'

And all the time everyone had to keep stepping over the totem pole. It still lay half in the hall and half in the sitting-room, for there was nowhere else for it to go.

'James,' said Grandmother at last, 'we'll simply have to find a home for it somewhere.'

Simon, who was sitting on it, gave the pole a gentle pat.

'But it's got a home,' he said.

'*I* mean a home that fits it,' Grandmother said firmly.

Great Uncle James rubbed his head and looked embarrassed. 'Oh. Ah – yes,' he said. 'Wasn't going to tell you yet – '

'Tell me what?' asked Grandmother.

'I expect it's another surprise.' Simon waited hopefully.

'You see,' said Great Uncle James, 'I've bought a house. You'd like it. Lots of room, with a nice bit of land round it. What's more, it's right in the middle of some proper old English countryside.'

'A house!' Grandmother was flabbergasted.

Great Uncle James nodded. 'Want to settle down,' he said. 'Might even do some farming. Don't know. Lots of plans. The thing is – would you come too?'

'To live in it? In the real country? Oh, *James*!' Grandmother clasped her hands together and began to smile. 'I should like it more than anything,' she said.

Simon let his breath out with a rush.

'*Now* you'll have somewhere to put your family tree,' he told Grandmother. He looked at the totem pole wistfully. 'I expect you'll be able to find a very interesting place for it.'

'Supposing we wait till the next time you come to stay,' suggested Grandmother, 'then we can decide about it together. Will that be all right?'

Simon looked at them both. Then he smiled.

'My goodness, *yes,*' he said, 'it certainly will.'

17 Simon makes a journey

Simon was sitting in a train. His mother had put him in at the beginning of the journey, and his big kind Grandmother was to meet him at the end of it. In the compartment, as well as Simon, was a tall lady with her two little girls. She had promised to see he was ready when it was time to get out.

The little girls had long narrow legs which reached down to the floor. Simon's legs swung to and fro, and he looked a very roundabout kind of person sitting beside them.

By lunch time, everyone was talking quite a lot. The tall lady had taken off her hat. Her hair sprang about in a free and easy way. They all exchanged sandwiches, and Simon told them about his grandmother being so good at football. The little girls seemed rather surprised.

'My Grandmother's quite good at *everything,'* said Simon. 'She does a lot of jumping,' he added, 'and she's a very good bowler. We once won a pig called Arthur.'

By the end of the journey everyone was very interested to have a look at Simon's Grandmother. The little girls' noses were pressed hard against the window as the train drew to a standstill in the little country station.

'Can you see her?' they said eagerly.

There was a pause.

'Yes,' Simon said suddenly, 'I *can,* and I think she's seen *me.*' His face grew pink as he struggled with the door handle.

Then a man opened it from the other side and a loud 'coo-ee!' echoed through the station.

Simon watched as the familiar figure came rapidly towards them with long swift strides. His Grandmother was taller than most of the other people. This was lucky, for she was happily twirling a stout walking stick around her head. Simon jumped down on to the platform as she reached him.

'Ho-ho-*ho!* There you are, Simpey!' said Grandmother, beaming down at him.

'Ho-ho-ho, I *am,*' smiled Simon.

Then, just for a moment, he got lost inside the yards of brightly coloured tweed that seemed to be wrapped round Grandmother.

'What a very floaty sort of coat,' Simon said, when he came out again.

'It's a cloak,' said Grandmother. 'It's very useful for all sorts of things. Now,' she said briskly, 'where's your case?'

They both thanked the tall lady, and waved to the two little girls when the train moved off again.

'Come along,' said Grandmother, 'Great Uncle James is waiting for us outside.'

The old-fashioned open car was resting comfortably in the road behind the station. Its yellow paint was sparkling with polish. Sticking out of the back seat was a large bristly sweeping brush with a long handle. Great Uncle James

heaved himself out of the driver's seat when he saw them coming. He smiled and stretched his arms as though they'd been waiting a long time. Simon thought he looked bigger than ever.

'Nice to see you boy.' His Great Uncle bent down and, grasping him under the arms, whisked Simon into the back seat of the car as if he was made of air.

'Hallo, Great Uncle James,' gasped Simon, 'I think you've put me on top of all your shopping.'

'No matter.' His Great Uncle took the case from Grandmother and ushered her into the front seat. 'Quick as you can, Kate,' he said. 'I could drink a bucket of tea.'

'Golly,' said Simon under his breath. He wriggled himself down in between the parcels.

Grandmother fitted her stick in a corner and arranged herself inside her big cloak.

'Hold tight!' she cried over her shoulder, 'I think we're off!'

'Don't like the look of the weather,' remarked Great Uncle James.

There was a grinding grating noise, followed by a loud bang, and the car gave two little jumps. Great Uncle James muttered 'come on, come on,' into his muffler. Then, suddenly, they were moving, gathering speed, with the hedges going by at a great rate.

'We're on a fiery charger,' Simon said with satisfaction. 'I expect we'll go like the wind.'

Soon they had left the station far behind. The car rattled along the country roads and Grandmother's cloak began blowing and billowing around her.

'You look like a parachute,' Simon said. He poked bits of it in from behind but it always billowed back again.

They turned a corner rather sharply and the long bristly brush fell across the back of the car. Simon grabbed it hastily. He felt himself sliding backwards among the parcels as the car began climbing a long steep hill. Grandmother turned to look at him.

'Good gracious,' she exclaimed, 'you seem to be in rather a muddle, Simpey.'

'It's the brush.' Simon moved the bristles away from himself. 'I've just rescued it.' Then he added, 'And it felt like fifty hedgehogs.'

Grandmother chuckled. 'Hang on,' she said, 'we'll be home in a brace of shakes.'

But the car began to go slower and slower as it mounted the hill. It was practically crawling along when it finally reached the top and the road was flat again. Great Uncle James breathed loudly through his nose.

'*Good* old girl,' he said. He began whistling a little tune as they gathered speed once more.

Simon had just got himself sitting up straight again when a large ginger cat suddenly shot out of the hedge and began to cross the road in front of them. Great Uncle James acted with speed. He sounded the horn, put on the brakes, and steered the car rapidly on to the grass bank at one side. The engine made a coughing sound and stopped.

'Well done, James,' Grandmother said calmly, 'you missed it.'

'What a nice little cat that was,' said Simon. 'I wonder where it's gone?'

Great Uncle James didn't answer. His face was a hot brick-red colour, and he didn't look at all pleased. He pressed the starter on the car, but nothing happened. He did this several times. Then he jumped out and peered under the bonnet.

'Cha,' he said crossly, 'she's not going to go.'

'I expect she got a fright with the cat,' said Simon.

'James,' Grandmother said thoughtfully, 'the farm is only just round the corner. Perhaps you could borrow a hearty man to help to push us off the bank? Then it's downhill all the way home.'

So Great Uncle James set off up the road.

'I expect he won't be long,' said Simon, 'he's got very tall legs.'

'That's just as well,' said Grandmother, 'for here comes the rain.' A crowd of fat raindrops began bouncing off the car bonnet. 'Great ducks and drakes,' she exclaimed, 'we shall soon be soaked!'

'I'm nearly soaked already,' said Simon. 'It's a pity this car hasn't got a top.'

'Half a moment,' Grandmother was heaving her big cloak out from underneath herself. Then she took it off altogether. 'Quick,' she said, 'you hold the brush up straight, with its leg on the floor.'

Swiftly she reached over and draped one end of the the thick material around the long bristles. Then she stretched the rest of it across to the front of the car. She looped one corner round the windscreen, and held up the other with the handle of her walking-stick. There was just room for the two of them to fit in underneath it.

'You've made a tent,' said Simon. 'What a very clever plan. I think I'm nearly dry already.'

'Good,' chuckled Grandmother, 'but hold on to the brush, or it'll all collapse on top of us.'

The rain had almost stopped and they were both quite dry when at last Great Uncle James arrived back with the farmer.

'Thought you'd be afloat,' he said.

'Grandmother's cloak is a very useful thing,' said Simon. They both came out from underneath it.

Then Grandmother grasped the steering wheel and pointed the car towards the road. Great Uncle James and the farmer gave a mighty heave from behind and Simon pushed himself backwards and forwards to help it

along. Soon the yellow car was back on the road again. They all waved to the farmer.

'Many thanks,' cried Great Uncle James. He jumped in as Simon and Grandmother began rolling away down the gentle slope.

Grandmother dangled her cloak outside the car to dry. 'The house,' she said, 'is around the very next corner.'

But Simon was thinking of something else. He was wondering if Great Uncle James really *would* drink his tea out of a bucket, now that he lived in the country.

18 The family tree

'I expect we'll soon go outside to look at everything,' Simon suggested the next morning. Great Uncle James had already gone off to the garage to mend his car.

'Of course,' said Grandmother. 'Can you find our boots? Then I'll be ready to come.'

So Simon ran into the little cloakroom where Grandmother and Great Uncle James kept all their outdoor things. It was full of big coats and clumpy shoes. There seemed to be golf clubs all over the place. Simon had a look at several of them.

When he got back with the boots Grandmother opened the kitchen door. This led out into a small green orchard. There was a flinty path that wound through the grass towards a neat white gate.

'Are you ready for the fray?' asked Grandmother. 'I've a lot to show you.'

They both had to thump their feet about to get their boots on properly.

'You've got some very curly apple trees,' Simon said, as they went outside, 'and miles and miles of garden.'

'I think I'll be a signpost,' Grandmother decided, 'then you'll see the lie of the land.'

She put her feet together and stuck both arms out straight on each side. Her right arm pointed at the back door.

'If you went through the kitchen till you came out at the other side, you'd be in the front garden,' she explained. 'You can see that bit from your bedroom.'

'I noticed a very good view of far away from my window,' said Simon.

'Yes,' agreed Grandmother. 'And *this* way,' she waggled the fingers of her other hand, 'you can see our back gate. That opens on to the lane, and there's a farm at the end of it.'

'How about where your nose is pointing?' asked Simon.

'That's the green jungle,' said Grandmother. 'The garage is there, as well as Great Uncle James's special workshop.' She lowered her arms and looked at Simon. 'Now,' she said, 'which way? You choose.'

'Well, first,' Simon said thoughtfully, 'it would be nice to see the Red Indian totem pole that Great Uncle James brought back from Canada.'

A strange expression crossed Grandmother's face.

'You said you'd be needing me to help you find a proper home for it,' Simon reminded her.

'Aha,' Grandmother paused. 'We could go to the farm,' she suggested. 'They've a fine selection of animals there.'

'I wonder where the totem pole *is* exactly?' said Simon, 'I didn't see it inside the house.'

Grandmother chuckled suddenly. 'All right,' she said,

making for the garage. 'I think I know where it might be.'

On the way they passed Great Uncle James's legs which were sticking out from beneath his yellow car. There were a great many tools lying about. They found the totem pole at last, half buried in some long grass behind the garage. The curious carvings on it looked very strange, staring up at them.

'It's a good thing we looked for it now,' said Simon, 'or it might have got lost for ever.'

'Yes,' said Grandmother slowly, 'it might.' She looked at it for a moment. 'I'm afraid we'd need an elephant to move it,' she said.

At once Simon said, 'Great Uncle James is *nearly* as strong as an elephant. I'll go and ask him.' He was off in a flash.

Presently he returned with Great Uncle James, who was wiping his hands on a rag and making a few grumbling noises. His face cheered up when he saw the totem pole.

'Bless me,' he exclaimed. 'How did that get here?'

'It must have been the removal men,' said Grandmother.

'And now we're going to find it a home,' said Simon. He looked down at the pole. 'Who's going to carry which bit?' he asked.

In the end, with a grunt and a heave, Great Uncle James grasped it round the middle and wrenched the totem pole out of the grass. Grandmother held on to the back end, and Simon was at the front. He had to keep his arms above his head to reach it.

'Lead on, boy,' growled Great Uncle James. 'Can't waste all morning.'

At once Simon guided the party past the garage, across a path, round the house and into the front garden. He stopped beside the smart white front door.

'I'm letting go,' he gasped, 'I think this is a *very* good place to put it up.'

Great Uncle James swung the pole upright and rested one end on the stone paving.

'Capital!' he exclaimed. 'What do you think, Kate?'

The sunlight shone brightly on the strange foreign faces that decorated the pole. They seemed to be glaring at everything. Wispy bits of grass were still clinging to it here and there.

Grandmother closed her eyes for a second before answering.

'I'm not sure,' she said faintly. 'You don't think it's rather . . . er . . . cross-looking to have beside the front door?'

'But it's your family tree,' said Simon. 'Great Uncle James said the Red Indians always put theirs in front of *their* houses.'

Grandmother brightened up suddenly. 'But we can't possibly have it there, James, because of the stone paving. It's much too thick to make a hole in.'

'That's true.' Great Uncle James rubbed his chin.

'But,' said Grandmother, 'it *could* go round the back into the orchard; that would be much easier.'

'Hum.' Her brother considered this. 'Pity the colours have faded,' he said. 'It ought to be in the sun to be seen properly. Still, perhaps you're right.' He swung the pole down again and spoke to Simon. 'Lead on again, boy. Let's go and see.'

'Oh goodness,' Simon said as they all set off again, 'I hope my arms won't be too tired to get there.'

He began by leading them into the centre of the front lawn. But Grandmother said the pole might frighten the cows in the next field if it was put there. When they swung round towards the back of the house, he suggested putting it beside the kitchen door.

'Then you could look at it all the time you were cooking,' he told Grandmother.

'I've just thought of the very place,' said Grandmother firmly. 'Follow me and I'll show you both.'

They all turned round and this time *she* led the way.

They went charging between the apple trees to the far end of the orchard.

'Whoa!' Grandmother stopped. 'If we put it in here,' she said, digging her heel into the ground, 'it'll have these three little fir trees for company.'

'Fine,' said Great Uncle James, who was tired of running round the garden, 'I'll dig a hole this afternoon.'

'It's a very dark green place for it,' objected Simon. 'You won't be able to see it properly unless you visit it.'

'We can't have it all ways,' said Grandmother briskly. 'Besides, it's the sort of place it grew up in, and we want it to be happy.'

Great Uncle James was a very quick digger, and soon after lunch the totem pole was comfortably settled in, among the little trees. It was still nearly as tall as a lamp-post. Simon decided to sit on the kitchen doorstep and look at it, so Grandmother went inside for a while.

Then Simon suddenly thought of something, and he ran at once to find Great Uncle James. Much later, when he came in for tea, he was smiling and smiling.

'I've got something to show you,' he said.

'Surprise, surprise,' exclaimed Grandmother. 'Whatever can it be?'

'Look out there!' said Simon. He flung open the kitchen door and pointed.

The totem pole had suddenly come alive with startling colour. In vivid greens and reds and yellows, the grinning faces gleamed and shone at them from the far end of the garden.

'Goats and monkeys!' said Grandmother, staring. 'Whatever has happened to it?'

'I knew you'd like it,' Simon said. 'Great Uncle James helped me with the top bits. He's got *hundreds* of paints in his little workshop.'

'Has he?' said Grandmother.

'Now you *can* have it all ways,' Simon said. He stood beside her in the doorway and smiled up at her. 'Our family tree is in a happy little spot – *and* we can see it properly as well.'

Grandmother's eyes began to twinkle. 'You're perfectly right,' she said. 'After all, what's the good of having a totem pole if you can't see it?'

Simon looked pleased. 'That's just what *I* thought,' he said.

19 False alarm

Great Uncle James had gone away for a few days, so Simon and Grandmother were all by themselves. That evening, Grandmother had one of her good ideas.

'How about a jaunt into town tomorrow, Simpey?' she suggested. 'I need one or two things I can't get in the village.'

'Oh yes,' agreed Simon. 'We might have an adventure.'

'You never know,' said Grandmother. 'We'll catch the early bus; it starts from the end of the lane.'

But they nearly didn't catch it at all.

The next morning, Grandmother slept far longer than she meant to. She woke with a start and looked at her watch.

'Bats and belfrys!' she exclaimed. 'We'll have to get a move on or we'll miss that bus.'

She leapt out of bed and hastened in to waken Simon. Then they both took it in turns to rush in and out of the bathroom. Very soon they were ready to go.

'No time for breakfast,' panted Grandmother. 'We'll take it with us.' She seized two bananas from the fruit bowl. 'We'll have another little something when we get there,' she added. Then she slammed the back door behind them. 'Come along.' She grabbed Simon's hand. 'We'll have to fly like the wind.'

Her gaily coloured cloak blew out behind her as they dashed along.

'My feet are nearly not touching the ground,' gasped Simon.

As they reached the end of the lane, they saw the little single-decker bus. The driver was just getting in.

'Ahoy,' croaked Grandmother, 'don't go without us.'

But the driver had seen them. All the passengers nodded and smiled as Simon and Grandmother climbed aboard. They were puffing and blowing like a pair of steam engines. When the driver had given them their tickets, the bus started off with a hefty jerk. Grandmother nearly sat down on Simon.

'Help!' he exclaimed. 'What a very squashy seat.'

When they'd recovered, Grandmother passed him a banana.

'I've never had breakfast in a bus before,' Simon said.

'A banana is a good thing for travelling,' said Grandmother. 'It's a nice tidy fruit.'

While they were eating, she had a little chat with some of the passengers.

After a while Simpey said, 'My banana skin is looking very draggly.' So Grandmother put it in her hold-all beside the other one. As the bus joggled along Simon remarked, 'It was funny about you not waking up.'

'I've been thinking of that,' said Grandmother. 'What we need is some kind of alarm clock. Just imagine, with

Great Uncle James away we might have slept till tea-time.'

Simon looked interested. 'I expect we could get a nice loud alarm clock in the town,' he said.

'That's a very good idea,' nodded Grandmother. 'We'll see about it directly we get there.'

The bus put them down in the town's ancient market place.

'Now for a clock shop,' said Simon at once.

They found a very good one in the main shopping street.

'Everything is ticking and tocking in here,' Simon said, as they went inside.

Grandmother spoke to the man behind the counter and told him what they wanted. He brought several alarm clocks to show them. 'What a splendid collection,' said Grandmother. 'I don't know which to choose.'

Simon looked at the man. 'We'd like a really loud one,' he said. 'My Grandmother's not very good at waking up.'

Grandmother's eyebrows went up. 'I'm not the only one,' she said. 'Perhaps we could hear some of these before we decide?'

So the man wound up the clocks and started them ringing, one after the other. Simon shut his eyes to pretend they were trying to wake him up.

'Well,' said Grandmother, when they'd finished, 'what do you think?'

'I think it would be better if they were a bit more clangy,' Simon said. 'I was *nearly* still asleep just now.'

‘Um,’ Grandmother said thoughtfully. She went for a little wander round the shop.

‘I’ve got one here,’ said the man. ‘It works with a battery inside it. It’s got a very loud ring which doesn’t stop until someone switches it off.’

‘That sounds just the thing,’ said Grandmother briskly; ‘then if *I* didn’t wake up, I expect someone else would hear it.’

‘I expect *I* would,’ said Simon. He looked pleased. ‘Then I could switch it off for you.’

The man put a shiny red clock on the the counter.

‘I’m afraid the paint is a little chipped on one corner,’ he said, ‘so we’re selling it very cheaply.’

'Better and better,' said Grandmother. 'I wonder what kind of a noise it makes?'

The little red clock was splendid. Grandmother and Simon both jumped with surprise when the alarm bell started. It rang so loudly that the clock bounced itself up and down on the counter. Several passers-by looked in through the window. Simon smiled broadly as he listened to it, till Grandmother nodded violently and the man turned it off.

'Wonderful!' she said. 'It would wake an elephant! We'll take it.'

'Golly,' agreed Simon, 'it would.'

The man kindly turned the clock round to show Grandmother how the knobs worked on the back.

'You're a nice noisy little thing,' Simon said to it. 'You can wake us up tomorrow.'

Then the man went to fetch a box and Grandmother began exploring the hold-all for her purse. Simon reached a hand up and felt one of the knobs on the clock. It went round quite easily. So did the other one.

'At last,' said Grandmother, producing her purse. 'It was hiding among the banana skins.'

It wasn't long before the clock was parcelled up and paid for. The man had kindly wrapped it in blue paper. He used a lot of sticky tape all over it. Simon said he would carry it, and they marched off to finish their shopping.

They bought a packet of coloured crayons and some knitting wool, and three yards of material to make curtains. Then they thought it would be nice to buy Great Uncle James a small present. After a lot of looking, they bought him a golf-ball with a tiny parachute attached to it.

'He can use it for practising his shots,' said Grandmother. 'The parachute will stop the ball from vanishing into the blue.'

'What a very good idea,' Simon agreed. 'And it will stop *me* from helping to look for them all the time.'

After that they went into a small café for some extra breakfast. Simon handed the clock to Grandmother.

'I expect you'd like to have a turn at carrying it now,' he said.

'Gracious,' Grandmother exclaimed. She looked at the bulging hold-all. 'Something will have to come out if this has got to go in.'

In the end Simon said he would carry the crayons. He began to walk rather slowly.

'Shopping is quite nice when you're not doing it *all* the time,' he said.

'But we've finished,' Grandmother said gaily. 'We're catching the very next bus home.'

It was quite a family party on the bus. All the same people seemed to be going back again.

'My word,' Grandmother said, 'I'm glad to sit down.' She squeezed the hold-all in under her seat.

'My word, so am I,' said Simon. 'I think I'll count my crayons.'

They were nearly half-way home when he noticed that Grandmother's head was nodding gently up and down. And at that very moment, two things happened. Grandmother made a sharp little snory noise. As if it was a signal, their new alarm clock suddenly came to life and started ringing, loud and clear, from underneath the seat. Grandmother jumped as if she'd been stung.

'Mercy me,' she gasped, 'what's up?'

Everyone in the bus was looking round. The alarm clock stopped for a short rest, then off it went again, ringing and ringing. The clamour was fearful. Simon giggled. Then he dived underneath Grandmother and struggled up again, holding the blue paper parcel. The ringing was louder than ever. Now and then the clock took a little rest and began again. Some of the passengers began to laugh.

'Cats and codfish,' muttered Grandmother. She struggled to open the parcel. 'It's this sticky tape,' she said. 'I could do with a pair of scissors.'

'I expect it'll finish in a minute,' a man said helpfully.

'It *can't* stop,' Simon grinned. 'It's got a battery. It'll be ringing for ever and ever.'

The noise went on and on while Grandmother pulled and tugged at the tape. Suddenly she began to laugh. She laughed so much that she couldn't even try to open the parcel. Soon most of the passengers were laughing too, bowing their heads and mopping their eyes, until, with the alarm clock still ringing merrily, the bus suddenly slowed down and stopped.

'Now then,' the driver made himself heard through the din, 'what's going on?'

He came down the bus, opening a pen-knife, and grinning widely at everyone.

'Let's have a go at that parcel,' he said.

He had it open in a jiffy. Grandmother took the clock

CY DOOR

from its box and turned off the bell. A great sigh of relief echoed round the bus.

'Thank you very much, I'm s . . . so sorry,' Grandmother said, her voice still rather quavery.

When the bus had started again, she began examining the clock.

'My *word*,' breathed Simon, 'I *said* we might have an adventure.'

'So you did. But what I can't understand,' Grandmother said slowly, 'is why it started at all. I suppose someone must have twiddled the knobs by accident.'

Simon looked at her suddenly.

'Yes,' he said thoughtfully, 'I suppose they must.'

20 An unexpected visitor

'We'll go to the farm for some eggs this morning,' Grandmother said. 'I'll just sweep up these crumbs first, because of the mice.' She dashed the broom around the kitchen floor.

'What mice?' asked Simon. He looked under the table hopefully.

'The mice who'll be popping in if I leave any crumbs about.' Grandmother nodded solemnly. 'You get a lot of unexpected visitors in the country,' she said.

It had been raining hard in the night, and there was thick mud at the farmyard gate. Simon was wearing his shiny new wellingtons.

'Gracious me!' cried Grandmother, 'There's a puddle here as big as a pond!' She gave a mighty leap and landed safely on the other side of it.

'I'll squidge through it,' Simon said. 'My boots will keep me quite dry.'

'Let's hope so,' said Grandmother. 'Now, let's go and find Mrs Tippett.'

The farmer and his wife lived in an old grey stone house that rambled all round the farmyard. It had some green grass in the front garden, with a fence and a gate to keep the farm animals out. Mrs Tippett was busy feeding a little cluster of chickens on the lawn. She peered over the tops of her spectacles as Grandmother and Simon came up the path.

‘ ’Morning,’ she said, ‘come for some eggs, have you? Shan’t be a moment.’

‘Good morning,’ said Grandmother. ‘This is my grandson.’ She introduced Simpey. ‘I call him Simpey, but his real name is Simon.’

‘Yes,’ said Simon, ‘and this is my Grandmother.’

Mrs Tippett’s smile went in and out as though she

hadn't meant it to happen. 'Chick-chick-chick,' she said, scattering the last of the henfood.

Simon sat on his heels to get a good view of the chickens eating. 'These are very pecky little things,' he remarked.

Just then a loud mournful noise rose and fell upon the air.

'That sounds like Hilda.' Grandmother looked surprised.

'Goodness,' said Simon. 'It *sounds* like a foghorn.'

'It *is* Hilda,' said Mrs Tippett. 'She didn't seem too well yesterday, so we kept her in. She's going back in the field today, though.'

'Who *is* Hilda, exactly?' asked Simon.

Grandmother chuckled. 'She's rather a friend of mine,' she said. 'She talks to me when I'm gardening. Perhaps we could go and have a word with her? I think I know where she lives.'

'You do that,' agreed Mrs Tippett, 'and I'll have your eggs ready when you come back.'

Grandmother led the way round a corner of the farmyard. Suddenly she said, 'Follow me,' and darted inside a low white building. So Simon did.

'Here she is,' smiled Grandmother. 'Come and say hallo. She's a charming creature.'

Then Simon saw that he was inside a cowshed, and Hilda was a big, gentle-looking cow. She had long eyelashes and twitchy ears, and she was the colour of creamy toffee. She rolled her eyes at her visitors, then raised her head and gave a loud mooing welcome.

'Hallo, Foghorn Hilda,' Simon said.

Hilda clattered her feet about on the stone floor.

'Where are you going?' Grandmother called to Simon. 'She's a perfectly friendly animal.'

'I'm not going anywhere,' he said. 'I was only waiting in case you were coming.'

Hilda's face was very soft and gentle. After a while Simon went into her stall and stood beside Grandmother.

'Good old girl,' said Grandmother. She gave Hilda a slappity pat.

'Good old girl,' echoed Simon. He reached a hand up and touched Hilda's side. The cow mooed gently.

'Splendid!' said Grandmother. 'Now she's a friend of yours as well.'

Later on, when they'd said good-bye to Hilda, they both had a look round the farmyard. There didn't seem to be anyone about. Simon went inside a stable. He came out again rather quickly. 'There's a large snorting horse in there,' he said.

They met Rufus, the farm dog, and discovered a litter of kittens lying in a heap of straw. They spent some time stroking the kittens.

'If I lived on a farm I'd always be patting something,' said Simon.

'Alas!' said Grandmother at last. 'It's time to go, I want to make a special pudding for lunch.'

Mrs Tippett gave them a pile of fresh eggs in a basket. At the farmyard gate Simon said, '*I'd* better take the eggs if you're going to be jumping the puddles again.'

So Grandmother obligingly leapt over three big ones, and Simon carefully squidged his way through them with the basket. When they got home they became very busy making Grandmother's special pudding.

'I'll count the eggs if you like,' Simon offered.

'Just three will do, as Great Uncle James is away,' Grandmother said.

So Simon counted out three eggs and Grandmother broke two of them into a cup. Simon broke the last one for her.

'You're not supposed to put the eggshell in as well,' said Grandmother. 'I'll butter the baking tin while you're getting it out.'

The pudding was a great success when it was finished.

'I shall rest my knees for a while on the sitting-room couch,' Grandmother said when they had washed up. 'They're not bending very well after all that jumping.'

'*I'm* not bending very well after all that pudding,' said Simon. 'I'll bring my drawing book and draw you a rather good picture.'

It was a long time later when they both heard the thumping noise coming from the kitchen.

'Heigh-ho,' Grandmother said sleepily. 'There's someone at the back door.'

'I'll go and see who it is,' said Simon.

Grandmother heard the back door open. There was an excited squeak from Simon, followed by a noisy stamping sound. As she sat up hastily, Simon dashed back, his face bright red with excitement.

'I think you'd better come!' he gasped. 'It's your friend Hilda; she's in the kitchen and she's *much* too big for it!'

'What!' Grandmother was out of the room in a moment. It was true. Hilda stood in the middle of the kitchen floor placidly nibbling a corner of the tablecloth. Her tail gently switched about around the pots and pans. She mooed in a shy kind of way when she saw Grandmother.

'I didn't know *cows* came into your kitchen,' Simon said. He pulled the tablecloth away from Hilda.

'Nor did I,' said Grandmother, a little breathlessly.

She opened the back door wide and gave her visitor a stern look. 'Now then, Hilda, out you go.' But Hilda didn't move.

'She seems to like being here,' said Simon.

'Maybe,' said Grandmother, 'but there isn't room for all of us. The trouble is,' she added thoughtfully, 'she's too big to turn round. We'll have to push her out backwards.'

Grandmother placed one hand on the cow's nose and the other on her shoulder. Simon decided to stay well behind and push Grandmother.

'Ready?' she said. 'Hey-up! Back, Hilda, *back*!'

But Hilda took a lot of pushing. First she got one boney hip wedged against the door frame, then she danced her back legs about and got the other side stuck.

'Hold hard.' Grandmother was breathing loudly. 'We'll have to think of something else.'

Hilda waggled her eyelashes and blew down Grandmother's neck.

'She seems to like you,' said Simon.

But Grandmother was thinking. 'There's only one thing to do,' she said. 'If we can't get her out backwards, she'll have to come forwards. We'll lead her through the dining-room and out of the front door.'

'Through the dining-room? *Golly*!' said Simon.

'Pass me that tablecloth,' ordered Grandmother.

She tied the cloth round Hilda's neck and gave it a little tug. At once the cow moved forward.

'I'll open all the doors,' said Simon.

Hilda didn't mind going through the dining-room at all. She stopped to look at some apples in a dish on the table, but one loud 'hey-up!' from Grandmother got her going again. She lumbered into the hall where Simon had opened the front door as wide as it could go. Then, as they all trooped out into the front garden, Mrs Tippett appeared, running down the path.

'*There* she is,' she panted with relief. 'I'd only just put her in the field, too. Someone must have opened the gate.'

Then she paused. She watched Grandmother untying the tablecloth from Hilda's neck. 'She looked as if she was coming out of your front door,' she said doubtfully.

'She *was*,' said Simon, 'and she's been in the dining-room as well. I think she came to see Grandmother.'

'I think she did.' Grandmother smiled at Mrs Tippett. 'She got a little stuck in the kitchen, you see, but she'll be all right now.'

'She's a very charming creature,' said Simon.

'Yes,' said Mrs Tippett, looking at them both. 'I think perhaps we'd better be off.'

As Hilda trotted gaily away to be put in her field, Simpey and Grandmother went inside.

'It was very interesting,' Simon said. 'I suppose Hilda was one of the unexpected visitors you were expecting?'

'Bless my soul!' exclaimed Grandmother, 'so she was.' She grinned at Simon. 'But I didn't think the visitor would be quite such a big one!'

21 Washing day

Simon had just finished cleaning his teeth. He wondered how far the drips would fly if he shook his toothbrush out of the window. But as he did so he let go by mistake. The brush flew out of his fingers and landed in the big holly bush below.

'Oh help,' he said. Then he ran to find Grandmother.

It took them some time to rescue the toothbrush. When Simon had said 'ow!' for the fourth time, Grandmother suddenly had a good idea. She fetched her sturdy walking stick and waggled it about inside the holly bush.

'At last,' she said thankfully, as the toothbrush slipped out on to the ground.

Simon borrowed the stick for a moment to see if there was anything else left hiding in the holly bush. But there wasn't. When he had finished, he looked at the dirty marks all over himself.

'You'd think the rain would keep washing the bushes clean all the time,' he said.

'Lackaday!' exclaimed Grandmother, looking at him. 'It seems as if *we* shall have to do some urgent washing, and there's quite a pile already.'

'It's a very sunny day to be going inside to do washing,'

said Simon, poking the earth out of his toothbrush.

'It's always the same with my washing,' sighed Grandmother. 'I keep enjoying the garden and not doing it.' She stood for a moment thinking. 'In the olden days,' she said, 'people lived sensibly. When it was a fine day they took their washing to the nearest river and dashed it about in the water.'

Simon looked interested. 'What a very handy thing,' he said. Then he added slowly, 'If we took *our* washing and dashed it about in the stream, we wouldn't have to stay inside.'

Grandmother's eyes sparkled. 'What a splendid suggestion,' she said. 'We may as well go at once.'

'Good,' said Simon. 'I'll help you collect everything.' He darted off.

Grandmother chose an old towel and a yellow spotted cushion cover from the linen basket. She put them inside a carrier bag and gave it to Simon.

'We can practise with these,' she said. 'I'll see if I can find a piece of scrubbing soap.'

When she had gone, Simon counted the towel and the cushion cover again.

'There's not going to be very much washing to practise with,' he remarked. He decided to pop one or two more things inside the bag.

On the way to the stream, along the lane, they saw Mrs Tippett. Grandmother waved the bar of soap in a friendly way.

Simon explained. 'We're just off to dash our washing about in the stream,' he said.

'Well I never,' said Mrs Tippett. 'Isn't the washing machine working, then?'

'Ha – well,' said Grandmother. 'I may try that this afternoon. We thought we'd use up all this lovely sunshine first, in case it vanishes.'

'I see,' said Mrs Tippett, who looked as though she didn't. 'Good-bye then.'

'I don't expect we'll be needing the washing machine at *all*,' said Simon. 'Let's hurry up in case we meet anyone else.'

The little stream ran swiftly between two grassy banks. At the far end, it flowed round a corner and disappeared into a wood. Grandmother chose a pleasant little spot beside the water's edge.

'It's lucky we're nice and early,' she said. 'There's no one else about. Now,' she pointed, 'here's a nice flat stone for you to do the scrubbing on.'

'I'm not exactly sure how I have to do it,' Simon said.

'Give me the yellow cushion cover,' said Grandmother.

Then she dangled it about in the water to wet it properly. She spread it out on the flat stone and gave it a vigorous rubbing with the soap.

'Oof!' she gasped, as she thumped the cover up and down on the stone. 'You have a try, I'm not in a very bending mood today.'

So Simon began rubbing and thumping and dipping and swishing. And Grandmother sat down comfortably with her back against a tree.

'I'll just do a little thinking,' she said. 'You can interrupt me when you've finished.'

Simon was very busy for quite a long time. He spread out the towel and the cushion cover to dry on the grass. Then he began on the extra things he had put in the carrier bag. He arranged these in a tidy pile on the edge of the stone.

'Everything is getting very slippy,' he decided. He was right. He put the soap down for a second to squeeze some water out of his trousers. In an instant, like a live fish, it glided off into the stream and landed with a splash.

'Oh golly.' Simon got down on his front and looked into the water.

The soap had settled in a bubbly cloud on the bottom.

'All this washing is very wetting,' he said gloomily.

The wetness reached up to his elbow before he could feel the soap at the end of his fingers. As he did so, his arm nudged the little pile of washing on the stone. It toppled in to join the soap.

'Oh *golly*,' Simon said again. He stood up quickly and went over to Grandmother. 'Could you stop thinking for a minute?' he said loudly. 'Hundreds of Great Uncle James's socks are going for a little swim. I expect he'd like them to be rescued.'

'What!' Grandmother opened her eyes and sat up.

'It would be nice if we had a fishing rod,' said Simon.

'It would be nice if we had anything,' Grandmother said

grimly. 'How did they all get there?' She watched helplessly for a moment as several brightly coloured socks floated swiftly off into the distance.

As Simon explained, the first sock vanished round the bend.

'Hey,' cried Grandmother, 'wait for me!' She galloped off to try and catch it up.

'Hey,' echoed Simon. *He* galloped off to try and catch Grandmother.

When they caught up with them, most of the socks were huddled together in a little bend of the stream. Here the water was still and cloudy looking.

'What a very funny thing,' said Simon. 'They've all turned green.'

'I hope they'll all turn back again,' Grandmother said. 'I'm not sure if Great Uncle James would care for that colour.'

Simon went back for the carrier bag while Grandmother rescued the muddy green socks from the water.

'As I'm getting them out, you can carry them home,' she said.

'Oh help,' said Simon, 'they don't smell very nice.'

The bag made an interesting drippy pattern on the ground going back down the lane.

'I wonder when Great Uncle James will be home?' Simon asked suddenly, as they reached the gate.

Grandmother chuckled. 'There'll be lots of time to put the washing machine on first,' she said.

'I expect all that green will come out,' said Simon.

'I'm sure it will,' agreed Grandmother.

'And he'll be very pleased that all his socks have had two washes,' continued Simon.

'*Very* pleased,' said Grandmother.

Simon drew a deep breath. 'Thank goodness,' he said.

And then they both began to giggle and giggle.

22 A parcel for everyone

When Great Uncle James came home again, he brought two parcels, one for Grandmother and one for Simon. Grandmother's was very long and thin looking.

'Ho ho,' she said, 'what have we here? I suppose it isn't a flag-pole?'

'It's some more of Great Uncle James's surprises,' said Simon. He began at once to undo his parcel. After a while he said, 'It's funny how the string round a present is always so knotty.'

'I was just thinking the same thing,' agreed Grandmother.

Great Uncle James produced his big knife and snipped the string round both parcels.

'Come on, come on, open up!' he said, in his hearty deep-down voice.

'I just am,' said Simon.

He pulled the paper off and found a box. There were some very strange things inside it. There was a big piece of strong see-through paper, with a coloured picture of a large bird printed on it. The bird had a fierce face and its feathery-looking wings were spread wide apart, as if it was flying. As well as the bird, there were five thin sticks of different lengths, and a fat ball of string. Simon smoothed the picture out and looked at everything.

'It's very nice,' he told Great Uncle James.

Grandmother dropped her own parcel and came to look.

'Why, it's a kite,' she said. 'How splendid! That *was* a good idea, James.'

Great Uncle James said something that sounded like 'Huff-poo' and looked pleased.

'Wonderful,' Grandmother continued. 'We'll fly it high in the air, o'er hill and dale, on the end of the string.' She waved her arms up and down several times. 'It won't take a moment to fix together.'

'Golly.' Simon looked puzzled. 'How exactly do we get it up there?'

'Show you this afternoon,' said Great Uncle James. He bent down and began fitting the five sticks into some special knobs on the bird picture. 'Have to find a good stiff wind first,' he said.

'We could go in the car to the moors,' suggested Grandmother. 'There's plenty of wind there, and lots of room.'

'Just the ticket,' said Great Uncle James.

He fitted the last stick and then gave the bird to Simon. Now the picture was no longer limp and floppy. The sticks had made the bird's wings stand out stiffly, and it looked ready to fly off at any moment.

'Zoom!' said Simon. He waved it round in a big circle. 'Zoom, zoom!' The paper flapped and crackled above his head. Then he said to Grandmother. 'I expect you're wondering what's in *your* parcel?'

So Grandmother opened it up. Her brother had given her the biggest umbrella Simon had ever seen. It had a strong thick handle, and the umbrella part was brightly striped in colours of blue and green and orange.

'Rain and hailstones!' Grandmother looked delighted. 'Thank you, James. It's just what I need.' She opened it up a little way and smiled happily. 'It's big enough to keep a bus dry.' Then she paused and looked at Simon. 'Have we another parcel that needs opening?' she said.

'I'll go and get it,' Simon said at once. He ran to fetch the present they'd bought in town for Great Uncle James.

'That's *our* little surprise,' he said, handing it over.

Making a lot of 'humph' and 'ho' noises, Great Uncle James had the paper off in a twinkling. He seemed very delighted when he saw his special golf-ball with the parachute attached to it.

'Most kind,' he said.

'The parachute is to stop your ball flying o'er hill and dale,' explained Simon.

'Very useful.' Great Uncle James put the ball in one of his big pockets. 'I'll try it this afternoon.'

So later on, when they set off for the moors, everyone had brought their presents with them. Grandmother clutched her new umbrella.

'There might be a snowstorm,' she said gaily. 'Then we could all get under it.'

As they drove along, the countryside began to get wilder and grassier and more lonely looking. The road became rough and bumpy. Soon there was nothing to be seen but a flock of sheep in the distance.

'Stop, stop!' cried Grandmother. 'The very place.'

As the car stopped, Simon stood up. His hair began to ruffle about.

'The *very* place,' he said, looking pleased. 'It's got a nice rushy wind.'

Then they all got out. Grandmother carried her big umbrella over her shoulder. Great Uncle James marched off, carrying a golf club to hit his special golf-ball with.

'Just going to try a few shots,' he called. 'Back in a jiffy.'

Simon followed with his kite. The string was tied to it

and already the bird was beginning to flip-flap about.

'It's nearly flying,' he said. 'I'm having to hold it till I'm ready.'

'Do you want any help?' Grandmother asked him. Simon paused. 'Don't you want to try your new umbrella?' he said. 'I could be flying my kite while you were sitting under it.'

'Right,' said Grandmother, 'but take care it doesn't vanish into the sky.' Then she left him to begin.

But the bird couldn't decide whether it wanted to fly or not. It would rise a little way into the air, with Simon running in front of it, letting out the string. Then, suddenly, it would change its mind and dive straight down into the ground again. Up and down he ran, lifting and pulling at the string, but it was no use.

'Oh goodness!' He was out of breath as he rescued the kite for the tenth time from some prickly bushes. He went across to Grandmother. She was sitting happily under her huge umbrella, gripping it firmly and sheltering from the wind.

'This is very nice,' she said comfortably. 'How are you getting on?'

Simon looked gloomy. 'My string is getting very tangled,' he said.

'String is very muddling stuff altogether,' said Grandmother. 'Let's find the end of it and start again.' She closed her umbrella and got up.

So Simon straightened out the string while Grandmother rolled it into a ball. The bird lay flapping its paper wings on the ground. All at once, a strange thing happened. Somehow Grandmother pulled on the string and the bird began to rise. She pulled again and started to run. The kite went higher and higher, and she began running faster.

'Help,' gasped Simon, 'it's off into the blue!' He began to run as well.

But soon Grandmother was quite a long way ahead across the moor. Her arm stuck straight up and her skirts sailed out behind her. She let out more and more string.

'Hurray!' she kept crying. 'Hurray!'

Soon the kite was so high that Simon had to bend his head right back to watch it.

'Golly,' he panted.

Two cars travelling along the road drew up and stopped. The passengers put their heads out to watch.

'Hey!' Now Great Uncle James was galloping along behind Simon, brandishing his golf club. 'Well done, Kate,' he shouted. 'Keep it up!'

And Grandmother kept it up splendidly. She ran and ran, up and down the grassy slopes, often jumping over bushes and ditches, until suddenly she met the flock of sheep. They scattered in surprise. Then she stopped. The whole of the string was in the air except for the bit she had wound safely round one finger. The kite was now far away, flying smoothly and strongly all by itself.

When Simon and Great Uncle James arrived, they gazed upwards in amazement.

'My word,' exclaimed Simon, 'it's a hundred miles away.'

Then Grandmother gave him the string to hold. When she had tied it carefully round his hand, she flopped down and lay on her back in the grass.

'Oof!' she panted with relief. '*This* is the best way to watch a bird flying.'

Simon and Great Uncle James had lots of turns at holding the kite.

'It's like fishing, upside down,' decided Simon. All the time he could feel the bird tugging and tugging on the end of the string.

After a while they all decided to move nearer to where Grandmother had left her umbrella. She sat down under it again. Then Great Uncle James went off to practise a few more golf shots, and Simon stood holding his kite. Still the bird flew bravely, as if it was there for ever.

'I'm glad you're enjoying your present,' Grandmother smiled up at him.

'Yes,' said Simon, 'we're *all* enjoying our presents.' Then he smiled back. 'I'm glad we all got the right parcels,' he said.

23 The house-warming

'Brr,' said Grandmother one morning, 'there's a shiver in the air. Can you feel it?'

'Yes,' said Simon, 'I can. It's a nice day to have a fire in your interesting fireplace.'

'Just what I was thinking,' agreed Grandmother. 'Let's speak to Great Uncle James.'

The fireplace in the sitting room of Grandmother's new home was so big that Simon could stand on the hearth and put the top half of himself right inside the ancient chimney.

It had a big oak beam across the front, and the bricks were very small and old and sooty looking. So far no one had lit a fire in it, but Great Uncle James thought it would be a good idea.

'I know,' said Grandmother. 'We'll have a house-warming party. When it's blazing merrily, we'll make some toast on the old brass toasting fork.'

'I expect we'll need a ton of coal,' said Simon.

Great Uncle James shook his head. 'Logs,' he said. 'Proper thing for this fireplace. We'll go and saw some.'

'I think my rheumatism's coming on,' murmured Grandmother.

But Great Uncle James was already marching off, so Simon and Grandmother put on their coats and followed him into the garden. There was an old dead apple tree in the orchard. Great Uncle James fetched a large axe and a curious looking saw from his workshop. The saw was very long and it had a handle at both ends.

'What a very sharp-looking thing,' remarked Simon.

Soon Great Uncle James had chopped a short branch off the apple tree. He arranged it across a small sawing bench to keep it firm and steady.

'You two begin on that,' he ordered. 'I'll cut some more branches off.'

Grandmother and Simon were some time before they got the saw in the right position. They stood one on either side of the bench and each grasped a handle. Then they began to pull the saw to and fro across the branch.

'You seem to be doing a lot of running up and down,' Grandmother remarked after a while. 'Hold hard with both hands and dig your heels in.'

'It's very difficult to hold hard with you pulling me all the time,' gasped Simon.

Great Uncle James put another armful of branches down beside them.

'James,' said Grandmother, 'this is very exhausting. I could do with a little assistance. Perhaps Simpey could come round to my side and you take his handle.'

So Simon stood in front of Grandmother, and they both held on to one end of the saw. Great Uncle James only needed one big hand on the other. Everything was much quicker after this. When there was a good pile of tumbly

logs on the grass Simon blew his cheeks up and let his breath out with a rush. He looked at Grandmother.

'I expect you're hardly tired at all with me helping you,' he said.

'Hardly at all,' Grandmother agreed. She looked at his flushed face and chuckled.

'A log fire warms you twice,' she said, 'once when you saw it, and once when you burn it.'

'I don't expect there'll *be* time to burn it,' said Simon, 'if we're going to be sawing and sawing.'

However, Great Uncle James decided they had done enough. He filled a barrow with the apple logs and trundled them off towards the house.

'Thank goodness,' said Grandmother, 'now we can start thinking about the toast.'

But the fire was in an awkward kind of mood. Three times Great Uncle James had to clear it all away and begin again. He got very red-looking with all the bending down. Then, at last, with a little piece of coal to start it, the wood caught alight and began sending smokey fingers up the chimney.

'I'll blow at it if you like,' Simon suggested. He got his mouth ready.

'Not yet,' said Great Uncle James.

Then Grandmother came in. 'Ha,' she said, 'I see we're in Red Indian country. There must be some splendid smoke signals coming out of the chimney.' She flapped a tea-towel briskly to and fro in front of the fire. Two flames went out.

'Hey!' said Great Uncle James.

Simon decided to go outside and look at the smoke signals. These were getting very interesting. The thick grey cloud pouring from the chimney was looking denser and blacker at every moment.

'I wish there was an Indian to see it,' he said. 'It's probably making a rather exciting message.'

Soon there was a great umbrella of black smoke all over the garden. Then Simon suddenly noticed something else. 'Help!' he gasped, and darted inside.

There was a choking smell in the hall.

'Grandmother,' he called, 'I think you ought to come, the house has smoke coming out of its ears, and quite a good little fire at the *top* of the chimney.'

Grandmother charged out of the front door and looked upwards.

'Cats and blackbirds,' she cried, 'the chimney's on fire! James!' Her voice boomed loudly. 'Come along, action stations!'

Then everyone began rushing about. Great Uncle James called for wet sacks to put the fire out in the sitting-room. Grandmother said they hadn't any sacks. Simon wet a kitchen towel and brought that. Great Uncle James thought of using Grandmother's big cloak, but Grand-

mother took it away again. Then she had a good idea. She soaked the two big door mats in the kitchen sink and rushed them, dripping, into the sitting-room.

That did the trick. The burning soot sizzled helplessly beneath the mats until finally it went out and the smoke began to clear away. At that very moment, a small shining fire engine dashed along the lane, and stopped, clanging loudly, beside the front gate. They learned that Mrs Tippett at the farm had seen the smoke and telephoned for the fire brigade.

'Ridiculous!' snorted Great Uncle James. 'Only a little smoke. All under control.'

'Perhaps,' said Grandmother mildly. 'But it would be a good idea if they took a look at the chimney just in case.'

So the firemen did. Simon watched as they ran a tall ladder up the side of the house. He tried his feet on the bottom rung, and got himself rather dirty helping everyone. He was very interested in looking at the old bird's nest that had caused all the trouble in the chimney.

'Lucky it wasn't worse,' a fireman said cheerfully.

Then Grandmother suggested tea for everyone. Mrs Tippett had arrived to have a look, so there were a nice lot of people for the house-warming party. But they had to have it in the kitchen.

'Any more toast?' Grandmother asked, when the big plateful was empty.

Simon was looking at one of the firemen. 'It must be very nice to just *sit* on a fire engine,' he said.

'It must be very exciting to have a clang at that bell,' nodded Grandmother.

The firemen looked at each other and grinned. 'We could take you to the end of the lane,' one of them said.

Grandmother's eyes sparkled. 'Bless my soul!' she exclaimed. 'Could you?'

And they really could. Mrs Tippett looked very surprised as she watched Grandmother and Simon careering down the lane in the fire engine. It was a tight squash, but Simon sat on one of the firemen. They all made a great deal of noise, and even Great Uncle James shouted, 'Three cheers!' as they finally arrived back at the gate, with Grandmother beaming out of the window.

'I *think* some people saw me,' Simon said, when the fire engine had gone.

'There's a lot of mess to clear up,' said Grandmother, 'but it was a very exciting house-warming.'

'Yes,' agreed Simon, 'it was.' He smiled slowly. 'But I expect the house got a little warmer than you *really* meant it to.'

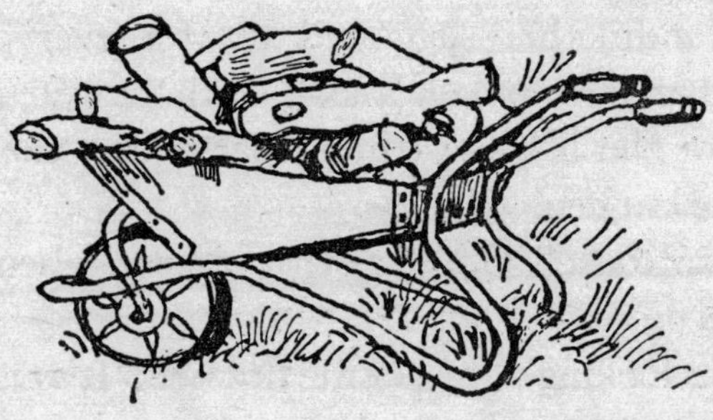

24 The invalid

Simon had only three days left of his holiday and he and Grandmother were deciding how to spend them. Great Uncle James thought he was starting a cold, so he had gone off to his workshop to snuffle by himself. Grandmother decided to straighten up his bedroom.

'I daresay he'll go back to bed,' she said. 'He gets very bad colds.'

Simon thought he'd have a look at everything.

'Great Uncle Janes has an enormous bed for one person,' he remarked.

'It's the biggest we could find,' said Grandmother, 'but he's not very pleased with the pillows; he says they're much too small.'

Simon was very interested in a string of Swiss cow bells on a leather strap that hung beside the fireplace. He spent a long time jingling them about.

'Keep a good look-out,' suggested Grandmother at last. 'We don't want more cows arriving at the back door.'

So Simon went to the window and kept looking, just in case.

'Rags and tatters!' Grandmother exclaimed suddenly. She was gazing at a big tear right up the middle of Great Uncle James's pyjama jacket.

'He's been doing his exercises again!' said Simon.

'We'd better mend it at once,' Grandmother said ruefully. Then her face brightened. 'I can use my new sewing machine,' she said. 'Wait till you see it; it works like lightning.'

The sewing machine was very exciting. It was an electric one, and Grandmother worked it rather cleverly by pressing a handle with her knee. Simon watched as she sat down and arranged the pyjama jacket underneath the needle. Then she took a deep breath.

'You'd better be ready to catch it,' she told him. 'I'm about to begin.'

As Simon stood waiting, her knee touched the handle. Instantly the jacket shot forward.

'Whoops,' said Grandmother, it's off without me.' Her hands were in a great hurry trying to hold the material straight.

'Whoops,' said Simon, 'It's like a busy bee. Bizzy-wizzy-wizzy,' he said. The needle flew down the seam, and the jacket fell into his hands.

Grandmother leaned over and snipped the threads. 'There,' she said proudly.

Simon looked at it. 'It went like *lightning*,' he agreed, 'and it's only a little bit squinty.'

Grandmother coughed. 'I'm not quite used to it yet,' she said. 'All I need is a little practice.'

'You could practise now,' Simon suggested.

Grandmother thought for a moment. Then she smiled slowly. 'There's a splendid arrangement for making button-holes,' she said. 'Fetch me a tea-towel and I'll show you.'

So Simon did, and Grandmother worked a neat little button-hole in each corner of it.

He considered it carefully. 'I suppose you could button it on to yourself when you're waiting to dry the dishes,' he said.

'So you could,' said Grandmother, 'and come to think of it, they'll be very useful little holes to hang it up by.'

'I'd better get some more,' Simon said straightaway, 'then they'll all have useful little holes, and it'll be nice for you to be practising.'

Grandmother got very good at making button-holes. She had just started on the fourth tea-towel when the sitting-room door opened and Great Uncle James peered in. His eyes looked droopy and his nose was very red.

'By code's worse,' he announced miserably. 'Ib go-ig to by bed.'

'Gracious,' exclaimed Grandmother. 'Off you go at once, and we'll bring you a hot water bottle.'

Her brother departed thankfully, and Grandmother and Simon bustled around, finding the bottle, and putting the kettle on.

'We'll take him a small tray of comforts,' said Grandmother. She put a steaming hot drink on it, a bottle of aspirin, and a big box of tissues. Simon added his rattly puzzle to give Great Uncle James something to do.

'You can carry the hot water bottle,' Grandmother said. 'But only as far as his door, because of the germs.'

For most of the day, Grandmother and Simon were busy keeping Great Uncle James comfortable.

There was his lunch to prepare, his hot water bottle to fill again, a book for him to read, another hot drink, and then his hot water bottle again. Simon blew up a balloon and tied it to his tea-tray.

'Perhaps he could play with that for a while,' he suggested.

But Great Uncle James was a very restless invalid. His voice became so hoarse and croaky with shouting for things that he had to rattle the string of cowbells when he wanted anything. He stayed in bed again the following day. Simon and Grandmother had just decided to go into the garden when the cowbells began rattling again. Grandmother marched upstairs once more. When she came down she shook her head in despair.

'It's his pillows,' she said. 'They're all on the floor again.'

'I expect he humps them off when he turns over,' said Simon. Suddenly he looked at Grandmother. 'It would be some more practising for you if you made him a special giant pillow on your new sewing machine,' he said. 'It would be too big to hump off, and then Great Uncle James would be nice and comfortable.'

Grandmother stared at him. 'Perhaps I could. Let's think a minute and make a plan.'

When they'd made it, she got up. 'I'll be back in a moment,' she said.

She took a measuring tape upstairs and measured all round Great Uncle James. He seemed rather surprised. Then she collected a very ancient eiderdown and part of an old sheet.

'Right,' she told Simon, 'let's get busy.'

'Bizzy-wizzy-wizzy,' said Simon. 'When are you going to work the sewing machine?'

Swiftly Grandmother cut two big squares out of the sheet. She machined these together, leaving a hole at one end.

'Hang on to that,' she ordered, 'I want to fill it up.' She slid her sharp scissors across the edge of the eiderdown. Instantly a cloud of tiny feathers burst out and floated everywhere. 'Quick!' Grandmother said hastily. She poked the cut end of the eiderdown inside the new pillow case and shook hard.

'Help,' gasped Simon, 'it's snowing feathers.'

'Don't let go.' Grandmother shook and shook at the eiderdown while Simon held tight to the pillow case. Gradually it began to fill up. There were feathers everywhere. Grandmother cut the eiderdown again. More and more feathers escaped.

'Poof!' spluttered Simon. 'Now I'm *eating* feathers.'

'Take no notice.' Grandmother waved one or two off her nose. 'We'll clear up later.' She chuckled loudly. 'This is going to be a remarkable pillow.'

And so it was. When it was full to the brim, and Grandmother had stitched up the hole to keep the feathers in, it was enormous. She had to put the eiderdown under the carpet to stop the rest of the feathers from coming out. Then she made a very smart cover for the pillow from a piece of orange curtain material.

The whole thing was so big and feathery that Grandmother and Simon could hardly see where they were going when they carried it upstairs. Simon watched from the door while Grandmother plumped it about behind Great Uncle James.

'*Barvelous!*' sighed the invalid, as he sank back into it. 'Very cubfortable id-deed.'

Simon and Grandmother had to use the vacuum to chase all the feathers downstairs. They had to give each other a little vacuum as well. And all the time they were clearing up, they only heard one sound from upstairs. It was a loud contented snore.

'Thank goodness,' smiled Grandmother later, as they went into the garden, 'I think he's comfortable at last.'

'I was wondering,' Simon said; 'if *I* caught Great Uncle James's cold I expect I'd have to stay here a bit longer.'

Grandmother chuckled. 'We'll go outside in the fresh air as much as possible,' she said. 'It's time we played some more football, too. That's the way to stop a cold coming.'

And it was.

The night before Simon went home, Grandmother came into his bedroom.

'I wonder what you and Great Uncle James will be doing when I'm not here,' Simon said gloomily.

'We'll save all the exciting things till you come back again,' Grandmother smiled.

'You could make us both a great big fat feathery pillow on your new sewing machine,' Simon suggested.

'So I could,' Grandmother agreed.

Simon smiled and yawned at the same time.

'Bizzy-wizzy-wizzy,' he said softly, and fell asleep.

Some other Young Puffins

The Shrinking of Treehorn
Florence Parry Heide

'Nobody shrinks!' declared Treehorn's father, but Treehorn *was* shrinking, and it wasn't long before even the unshakeable adults had to admit it.

Tales of Joe and Timothy
Joe and Timothy Together
Dorothy Edwards

Friendly, interesting stories about two small boys living in different flats in a tall, tall house, and the good times they have together. By the author of *My Naughty Little Sister* stories.

David and his Grandfather
Pamela Rogers

Three long stories about David and his kind, friendly Grandfather, who participates in all his secret schemes.

The Adventures of Uncle Lubin
W. Heath Robinson

The amazing adventures of good old Uncle Lubin in his search for his little nephew, Peter, who has been stolen by the wicked Bag-bird. With the author's own unforgettable illustrations.

Jacko and Other Stories
Jean Sutcliffe

Stories about pets and people by an expert who is really in touch with young children – the creator of the *Listen with Mother* programme.

Playtime Stories
Joyce Donoghue

Everyday children in everyday situations – these are stories for parents to read aloud and share with their children.

The Anita Hewett Animal Story Book

A collection of cheerful, funny, varied animal stories from all over the world. Ideal for reading aloud to children of 5 or 6.

Duggie the Digger and His Friends
Michael Prescott

As well as Duggie the Digger, there are tales about Horace the Helicopter, Bertram the Bus and Vernon the Vacuum Cleaner. It will please little boys who are interested in mechanical things.

Bad Boys

ed. Eileen Colwell

Twelve splendid stories about naughty boys, by favourite authors like Helen Cresswell, Charlotte Hough, Barbara Softly and Ursula Moray Williams.

My First Big Story Book
My Second Big Story Book
My Third Big Story Book

ed. Richard Bamberger

These three books contain a wonderful hoard of nursery rhymes and bed-time stories, ranging from traditional English favourites to strange new tales from other lands.

Time and Again Stories

Donald Bisset

It's rare to find nonsense stories as fresh and original as these. In Donald Bisset's world crows are called Albert and dream upside down, and words get caught in telegraph wires.

The Owl Who was Afraid of the Dark

Jill Tomlinson

Being afraid of the dark has its problems, especially when you're a baby owl, but Plop comes to learn that the dark can be exciting, fun, beautiful and a lot else besides.